George Orwell Studies

Volume Four

No. 2

George Orwell Studies

Publishing Office
Abramis Academic
ASK House
Northgate Avenue
Bury St. Edmunds
Suffolk
IP32 6BB
UK

Tel: +44 (0)1284 700321
Fax: +44 (0)1284 717889
Email: info@abramis.co.uk
Web: www.abramis.co.uk

Copyright
All rights reserved. No part of this publication may be reproduced in any material form (including photocopying or storing it in any medium by electronic means, and whether or not transiently or incidentally to some other use of this publication) without the written permission of the copyright owner, except in accordance with the provisions of the Copyright, Designs and Patents Act 1988, or under terms of a licence issued by the Copyright Licensing Agency Ltd, 33-34, Alfred Place, London WC1E 7DP, UK. Applications for the copyright owner's permission to reproduce part of this publication should be addressed to the Publishers.

© 2020 George Orwell Studies & Abramis Academic

ISSN 2399-1267
ISBN 978-1-84549-763-7

George Orwell Studies

Contents

Editorial
How the Spotlight is Increasingly Falling on the Powerful Women in Orwell's Life – by Richard Lance Keeble — Page 3

Papers
Orwell in Marrakech – by Kevin Carter — Page 7
Orwell's Aunt Nellie – by Darcy Moore — Page 30
Orwellian or Campbellian? 'Invisible Sources' in Orwell's 'Shooting an Elephant' and *Burmese Days* – by Carol Biederstadt — Page 45
Orwell's Evil-Scepticism – by Peter Brian Barry — Page 64
Orwell and Dress: The Naked Truth? – by Richard Lance Keeble — Page 78

Article
What If He Had Lived … or Waited? George Orwell and Counterfactual Biography – by John Rodden — Page 95

Re-evaluations
Stansky and Abrahams: Orwell's First Biographers – by Darcy Moore — Page 104

Letter
Masha Karp Answers her Critic — Page 115

Book reviews
Thomas J. Sojka on *A History of 1930s British Literature*, edited by Benjamin Kohlmann and Matthew Taunton; Polly Hember on *If George Orwell Were Alive Today: On Nineteen Eighty-Four and the Thrust of Orwellian Satire*, by John Dale; Jonathan Greenaway on *Red Britain: The Russian Revolution in Mid-Century Culture*, by Matthew Taunton, and Daniel Buckingham reviews *On Nineteen Eighty-Four: A Biography*, by D. J. Taylor — Page 117

Editors
Richard Lance Keeble — University of Lincoln
Tim Crook — Goldsmiths, University of London

Reviews Editor
Megan Faragher — Wright State University

Production Editor
Paul Anderson — University of Essex

Editorial Board
Kristin Bluemel — Monmouth University, New Jersey
Peter Marks — University of Sydney
John Newsinger — Bath Spa University
Marina Remy — Paris Sorbonne
John Rodden — University of Texas at Austin
Jean Seaton — University of Westminster
Peter Stansky — Stanford University, US
D. J. Taylor — Author, journalist, biographer of Orwell
Florian Zollmann — Newcastle University

EDITORIAL

How the Spotlight is Increasingly Falling on the Powerful Women in Orwell's Life

RICHARD LANCE KEEBLE

2020 marks the 70th anniversary of the death of George Orwell at the tragic, early age of 46. Not surprisingly, a number of special events are being organised: in particular, there's the publication of Sylvia Topp's long-awaited biography of Orwell's first wife, Eileen O'Shaughnessy (Unbound, 2020). A series of launch events and interviews around the country culminate with a weekend at the end of March in South Shields where a blue plaque will be unveiled at her childhood home, Westgate House, on Beach Road.

Eileen features prominently alongside Orwell in Kevin Carter's remarkably detailed essay about the couple's trip to Marrakech between September 1938 and March 1939 which opens this issue of *George Orwell Studies*. After being discharged from Preston Hall Sanatorium, in Aylesford, Kent, in August 1938, with suspected TB, Orwell was advised by his doctors (including Eileen's brother, Laurence) to take a break in a warm climate to help recovery. The Blairs were unable to finance a trip abroad but were offered an anonymous loan of £300 through friends Max and Dorothy Plowman. As Carter reports: 'They acted as intermediaries for writer, and fellow old-Etonian, L. H. (Leopold Hamilton) Myers, who had visited Eric at Preston Hall with the Plowmans. Eileen said Eric insisted that it was a loan and not a gift; he repaid the debt in 1946, through the then-widowed Dorothy Plowman, from the proceeds of *Animal Farm*. This was two years after the death of Myers, who took his own life in 1944. Even then Eric remained unaware of who had provided the loan.'

We learn much about Eileen's responses to her Moroccan adventure through the letters she sent to her friend Norah Myles, signed Pig, to writer Geoffrey Gorer and to Mary Common (wife of Jack,

Richard Lance Keeble

Orwell's friend from the *Adelphi* magazine) who was looking after their house and shop in Wallington while the Blairs were away. Letters from Eileen to Eric's mother, Ida Blair, also survive. Eileen read through the drafts of the novel, *Coming Up for Air*, and his essay on Marrakesh 'perhaps contributing the memorable opening line of Marrakech about the funeral procession, the flies leaving the restaurant in a cloud, rushing after the corpse, but coming back a few minutes later'. Eileen also did the cooking and the washing and cycled around the town on a red Japanese-made bicycle while shopping. They both cultivated a small garden and tended to the animals. They wandered through the bazaars, travelled into the nearby countryside and spent a week in the High Atlas Mountains. They also re-read the works of Charles Dickens – books again supplied by Francis Westrope – which provided the material for the essay, 'Charles Dickens', published in 1940.

Carter's essay is jam-packed with fascinating details about the trip. Along with the references, some 134 notes give an indication of the massive research involved. It is writing clearly inspired by a deep love for the subject.

As Orwellian scholarship advances, the focus is, indeed, increasingly turning towards some of the many powerful women in his life who have been for too long marginalised in the memoirs and biographies. Next, Darcy Moore puts the spotlight on Aunt Nellie who was certainly an important presence throughout Orwell's life. Delving deep into the archives (the Library and Museum of Freemasonry, Wandsworth Register Office, Ida Blair's diary, the British Library, Esperanto Archive, London Metropolitan Archives and so on), Moore brings together a wealth of information about Nellie's extraordinarily colourful life. For instance, he highlights the freemason background of many of her male relatives, her involvement with the Suffragettes, her time in jail, her acting career, her promotion of Blair's early writings through her contacts with radical intellectuals, her relationship with Eugène Adam, her involvement in the Esperanto movement, her tragic end just months after Orwell's death – and much more. Moore is right to argue: 'It is evident how profoundly she influenced and shaped her nephew's early literary and political experiences. Blair may never have travelled far down the path to becoming the writer Orwell without his Aunt Nellie's encouragement, support and literary contacts.'

In one letter, unearthed for the first time, from December 1949 and buried in the Esperanto SAT Archive, Nellie tells her Esperantist friend Lucien Bannier how, unlike many of Orwell's friends and family, she wholeheartedly approves of the 'very intelligent' Sonia Brownell as 'certainly a most suitable companion for Eric'. We can only imagine how important that opinion was to the dying Orwell given the fact that Aunt Nellie had been the source of constant support and intellectual stimulation throughout his entire life.

In a paper intriguingly titled 'Orwellian or Campbellian? "Invisible Sources" in Orwell's "Shooting an Elephant" and *Burmese* Days', Carol Biederstadt examines meticulously the themes of those two celebrated works. Comparing them with earlier texts by Reginald Campbell, she traces significant and indisputable similarities. And Biederstadt goes on to pose the inevitable question: 'Is it possible to explain these similarities away as sheer coincidence – the result of two men having similar experiences while serving in colonial Burma and neighbouring Siam – or does the uncanny resemblance of these texts suggest that Orwell's essay and novel may have been directly influenced by the works of Campbell?'

Orwell regularly speaks of evil. For instance, early in his service in the British Raj, he writes: 'I had already made up my mind that imperialism was an evil thing and the sooner I chucked up my job and got out of it the better.' Yet Peter Brian Barry argues here that Orwell is best seen as an 'evil-sceptic' – doubting whether there is very much evil in the actual world. Orwell implicitly offers three arguments for some version of evil-scepticism which are explored in detail. And Barry concludes: 'Perhaps surprisingly, a fair reading of Orwell's corpus suggests that he is deeply sceptical about the existence of evil and evil people.'

My own paper takes a look at Orwell's appearance and the representation of clothes (and nakedness) in his writings. What pleasure I had in researching this piece. A number of thoughts follow on. At one point I examine the photographs of Orwell to find out the kinds of clothes he prefers (ties, for instance). Another constant feature of Orwell's appearance I highlight is the pencil-thin moustache which he acquired while serving as an Imperial Policeman in Burma from 1922-1927 and kept for the rest of his life. Interestingly, no photograph of Orwell, as far as I can find, shows him reading. How strange, since Orwell was such a voracious reader. This addiction to books, this curiosity about life, this love of being immersed in imaginary worlds, emerges fully formed at Eton – and never leaves him. Perhaps all this reveals something about the intriguing conventions of photography – and how careful researchers must be when using photographs as the basis for studies of both individuals and societies: often the important can go missing.

Moreover, while in my essay I explore Orwell's fascination with dress it is interesting that he never examines the place of clothes in the books he reviews and comments on in his many essays. Can I then recommend Shahidha Bari's excellent *Dressed: The Secret Life of Clothes* (Jonathan Cape, 2019) which takes in the representation of clothes by writers as diverse as Roland Barthes, Sylvia Plath, Søren Kierkegaard, Henry James, Virginia Woolf, Nikolai Gogol, Brett Easton Ellis, T. S. Eliot and Samuel Beckett. Orwell wrote a wonderful

Richard Lance Keeble

essay on P. G. Wodehouse in which he argues that the creator of Jeeves and Wooster is no Nazi but – because of his political naivety – simply bamboozled into broadcasting from Germany during the Second World War. Nowhere does he ponder the representation of clothes. Bari, in contrast, in her fascinating section on Wodehouse and dress, comments:

> Although the formal nature of the master and servant arrangement structures the stories, it is a relationship of mutual and profound affection. Jeeves cares for Wooster's clothes and, by proxy, Wooster too, just as Wooster commands and yet depends on his servant's sagacity. Jeeves's unfailing judiciousness in matters of dress is a mark of his more general wisdom … (p. 99).

So we have Orwell's voice (Taylor, 2003), his cough (Ross, 2012), his nose (Sutherland 2016) and now his moustache (Keeble, 2020). What on earth will be next?

Richard Lance Keeble
University of Lincoln and Liverpool Hope University

Orwell in Marrakech

KEVIN CARTER

This account of Eric and Eileen Blair's time in Marrakech (from September 1938 to March 1939) focuses on the places where they stayed or visited and the people they met and mentioned. Much has changed in the eighty years since the Blairs visited Marrakech. The city has grown exponentially and the population of Marrakech now approaches one million. In recent years, Morocco – which Eric already considered debauched by international visitors – has embraced mass tourism, while resorts and golf courses proliferate, particularly to the south of the walled city. Only two of the places where the Blairs stayed remain immediately recognisable (and at the time of writing one is at risk of imminent redevelopment), but it is still possible to walk in the footsteps of the Blairs in the old city, in the French enclave of Guéliz and to travel (as they did) to Taddert in the High Atlas mountains.

BACKGROUND

In September 1938, Eric Arthur Blair – the real name of writer George Orwell – travelled with his wife Eileen (née O'Shaughnessy) to Marrakech to convalesce after treatment for bronchitis of the lung and suspected tuberculosis (Shelden 1991: 316-319). Eric had long suffered ill-health, saying that 'in winter, after the age of about ten, I was seldom in good health', adding that 'I had defective bronchial tubes and a lesion in one lung … and a chronic cough' (Orwell 1998, 19 [1952]: 368). His condition(s) could only have been aggravated by the austere environment at St Cyprian's, his prep school in Eastbourne, the heat and humidity of Burma, spending time down and out in Paris and London, on the road to Wigan Pier and in the trenches and streets of Aragon and Catalonia. Eric was a chain-smoker too and – after returning from Spain in 1937 – had settled with Eileen, back in a cold and damp cottage and store at Wallington, Hertfordshire, where they had married in the village church on 9 June 1936.

On 15 March 1938, Eric was admitted to Preston Hall Sanatorium, in Aylesford, Kent. While his doctors suspected phthisis (tuberculosis of the lungs), both Eric and Eileen thought they were being lied to. When discharged at the end of August his doctors, including J. B. MacDougall and Eileen's brother, Laurence O'Shaughnessy, coincidentally a chest and thoracic surgeon,[1] recommended that they rest and spend the coming winter in a warmer climate. Eileen felt they had been bullied into this decision, which would put Eric into debt for the first time in his life; Eileen went on to describe her brother as one of 'nature's fascists' (Davison 2006: 76).[2]

Necessarily avoiding Spain (and Spanish Morocco), where some of his former comrades in the POUM militia had been killed or imprisoned during the Spanish civil war, Eric and Eileen chose to go to Marrakech in French Morocco. Here, in September, the oppressive heat starts to give way to a mild and pleasant winter. Daytime temperatures average 33 degrees in September, falling to 20 degrees by December, when there are clear blue skies and occasional overnight frosts. Laurence O'Shaughnessy was also able to recommend a doctor in Marrakech.

Eric wrote to Francis Westrope, his former employer at Booklovers' Corner in Hampstead, asking for second-hand guide books and maps of French Morocco and a small Arabic dictionary, to enable them to pick up a few words of the language.[3] Eric confessed to Jack Common that he and Eileen thought that 'French Morocco gave on the Mediterranean, whereas really it's the Atlantic'.[4]

The cost of the journey was beyond their means, but they were offered an anonymous loan of £300 through friends Max and Dorothy Plowman. They acted as intermediaries for writer, and fellow old-Etonian, L. H. (Leopold Hamilton) Myers who had visited Eric at Preston Hall with the Plowmans. Eileen said Eric insisted that it was a loan and not a gift; he repaid the debt in 1946, through the then-widowed Dorothy Plowman, from the proceeds of *Animal Farm*. This was two years after the death of Myers, who took his own life in 1944. Even then Eric remained unaware of who had provided the loan.

Rest did not come easily to either Blair. While in Morocco, Eric completed the draft of his novel *Coming Up For Air*, the essay Marrakech,[5] kept political and domestic diaries, corresponded with friends, especially Jack Common who looked after the house and shop at Wallington, and reviewed a number of books. His diaries show that he took a particular interest in the local flora and fauna, farming methods and technology, as well as the egg production of his chickens, the politics of the region and attitudes to events in Spain and the coming war in Europe. He also kept a pocket notebook to record the prices of goods and services.[6]

While in Marrakech, Eileen had a lively and entertaining exchange of correspondence with friend Norah Myles, signed Pig, with Geoffrey Gorer and Mary Common, wife of Jack; letters from Eileen to Eric's mother, Ida Blair, also survive. Eileen read through the drafts of the novel and the essay, perhaps contributing the memorable opening line of 'Marrakech' about the funeral procession, the flies leaving the restaurant in a cloud, rushing after the corpse, but coming back a few minutes later. Eileen also did the cooking and the washing and cycled around the town on a red Japanese-made bicycle while shopping.[7]

They both cultivated a small garden and tended to the animals. They wandered through the bazaars, travelled into the nearby countryside and spent a week in the High Atlas Mountains. They also re-read the works of Charles Dickens – books again supplied by Francis Westrope – which provided the material for the essay, 'Charles Dickens', published in 1940.[8]

JOURNEY TO MARRAKECH

After leaving the sanatorium at the end of August 1938, Eric and Eileen briefly visited Richard Blair, Eric's ailing father, in Southwold, Suffolk, and spent one day in London, before beginning their journey to French Morocco. They travelled on the newly-built P&O ship, the *SS Stratheden*,[9] leaving Tilbury Dock at 6pm on 2 September, crossing the Bay of Biscay to Gibraltar. On the ship's manifest, Eric describes himself as a novelist, Eileen as having no profession; both gave their address as the Stores, Wallington.[10]

On the ship Eric avoided seasickness by taking a German remedy called Vasano.[11] He was well enough to spend his time correcting the French translation of his last book, *Homage to Catalonia*.[12]

They continued their journey to Tangier, where they arrived on 9 September. Their onward journey was delayed because ships were full, so they opted to travel to Casablanca by train, continuing on to Marrakech the following day. After an early morning start, they negotiated their way through various bureaucratic checks and a change of train at a mid-way junction,[13] where they lost most of their luggage, which they did not get back for weeks. Eric said that 'at every station there is an enormous horde of Arabs all literally fighting for the job of porter'.[14] Evidently, the baggage went astray in the melée.

They arrived at the main station at Marrakech which had opened fifteen years earlier in 1923; the original station was replaced by a stylish modern building in 2008.

HOTELS IN MARRAKECH

Eric and Eileen stayed initially at the Hôtel Continental on the Rue des Banques, within the Médina, the old walled city. The hotel was a five-minute walk from the Jemaa El Fna,[15] the main square, still the bustling heart of Marrakech. The hotel, which had been managed by a Monsieur Gonzales and then Monsieur Charles Plat, *Directeur*, had been recommended to Eric and Eileen.[16] Although

Eric did not notice, Eileen described it as a brothel and blamed *Cooks' Lists* for being a bit out of date.[17] In spite of its advertised 'very moderate prices'[18] they left after just one night.

They moved to the Majestic Hôtel on the Rue des Écoles, later Rue Clémenceau,[19] but now Boulevard El Mansour Eddahbi,[20] in *la Ville Nouvelle*, Guéliz. The name of the district is said to derive from the French word l'église – although another translation suggests it originates from a local word for sandstone, from which much of the city is built. To this day Guéliz is home to many of the large French community in the city. They began to settle in Marrakech soon after parts of Morocco became a French protectorate in 1912. Within six years the expatriate population increased from 30 (predominantly British) to 1,500, of whom 1,200 were French (Bennani 2017: 191). The protectorate lasted until 1956.[21]

Eileen described the Majestic as the second most expensive in Marrakech (the Mamounia,[22] which still exists, was probably more expensive), but calculated that it was much cheaper to have full pension here (95 Frs[23] a day for two), than to go to restaurants.

The art deco hotel, designed by architects Paul Sinoir and Robert Poisson, opened in 1928. They also designed a number of public buildings and the villa and studio of French artist Jacques Majorelle, later owned by Yves Saint-Laurent and partner Pierre Bergé, which is now a major tourist attraction. The hotel was later renamed the Koutoubia (after the largest mosque in Marrakech), but subsequent owners have allowed it to fall into ruin and it awaits redevelopment, most likely into a now permitted six-storey building, as opposed to the original two storeys.[24]

THE BRITISH CONSULATE

Eric and Eileen registered their presence with the local authorities and were issued with undated identity cards, most likely within the first few days of their arrival, at the *Hôtel de Ville,* Avenue du Guéliz, now Avenue Mohamed V, another building designed by Paul Sinoir. On Saturday 17 September 1938, Eric and Eileen made depositions at the British Consulate which was then located on Avenue Bab Djedid (Jdid). Here they met the Consul Robert Parr – who signed their depositions – and Vice-Consul Bryce James Miller Nairn, the unnamed member of a missionary family.

Eric wrote about Parr (and Nairn) in a diary entry dated 22 November 1938, following a meeting some days earlier. He described Parr as 'a man of about 40, cultivated, very hospitable, married, and in easy circumstances. Speaks French, very careful and grammatically very correct, but strong English accent and manner while speaking of, mentally going over the grammar rules'.[25] It is unclear why two Englishmen were speaking French, unless there were others present.

Robert Parr was actually 44 (born 15 May 1894) and his home addresses are recorded as Black Birches, Hadnall, and later Grinshill Hall, Grinshill, both near Shrewsbury. He served in the Serbian army during the First World War, allegedly having been turned down by the British forces because of poor eye-sight. He was later awarded the Order of the White Eagle (Serbia), Order of the Black Eagle (Albania), Gold Medal for Bravery (Serbia) and the Serbian Retreat from Albania Medal.[26]

He joined the Levant Consular Service in October 1919 and was initially assigned to Constantinople (Istanbul) in 1920 and later served in Durrazzo (Durrës, Albania), Damascus, Port Said and Aleppo before being appointed to Marrakech on 14 February 1937. He moved to Brazzaville on 28 October 1940 and concluded his career at Lyon, immediately after the Liberation, serving there from 1944 to 1955, retiring in 1956. He was awarded an OBE in 1927, a CMG in 1943 and a knighthood (KBE) in 1950.

Parr married Cicely Emily, née Shaw, in March 1918 at St George's, Hanover Square, in central London. Cicely had served first in the Kingsland Hospital as a Volunteer Aid Detachment nurse and later as an ambulance driver with a Scottish women's field unit in Macedonia. Invalided home in the early part of 1917, on her recovery she worked as a driver for the Air Ministry. She was later awarded the British and Victory medals. In 1924, she organised and carried out famine relief work in the mountains of Northern Albania while Robert Parr was serving in Durrazzo.

A few days after his meeting Eric, Robert Parr travelled to the UK and then back to Marrakech with his son, (Robert) Philip (1923-1944), a student at Winchester College, and daughter Gillian, later Livingstone-Learmonth (1925-1992), presumably for the Christmas holidays. Sadly, just six years later, Philip, by then a Lieutenant with the 6th Battalion, the Grenadier Guards, was killed in Italy in 1944. He is buried at the Commonwealth War Cemetery at Minturno, some 78 kilometres north of Naples. Sir Robert Parr KBE, CMG died at Stroud in 1979 and his wife, Cicely Emily, in 1964.

Eric wrote that 'the Assistant Consul or Vice-Consul is a young Englishman son of missionary, who has apparently been brought up in Morocco. Nevertheless has more characteristically English manner and accent than, eg an Englishman brought up in India'.

Bryce James Miller Nairn was born in Marrakech on 9 July 1903, the son of Cuthbert and Mary (née Miller) Nairn from Stewarton, Ayrshire. They, along with Cuthbert's sister, Jessie, were medical members of the South Morocco Mission, founded by John Anderson (Fiedler 2018: 226) – the organisation predated the arrival of the French Protectorate. Alan Lennox, the long-serving British Consul at Marrakech (until 1920), was also a missionary. On 9 November 1944, Cuthbert Nairn was murdered by a native in Marrakech, a few weeks before retiring back to Scotland.[27] He is buried in the European Cemetery in Marrakech.

After completing his studies in Scotland, Bryce Nairn returned to Morocco in 1927 to work as a veterinary surgeon. He travelled with his wife, Margaret (née White), a professional painter, and recently-born daughter Jill. Sadly, Jill died in Marrakech in 1933; a second child, Barbara, was born in Pollok, Scotland, in 1935.

Bryce was employed at the Consulate at Marrakech from 6 July 1933 and was acting Consul there in 1936 and again in 1938. He was appointed Vice-Consul on 15 July 1938, shortly before meeting Eric and Eileen. He continued his career in the Consular Service, transferring to Tangier in 1940 and later served in Brazzaville (1941) seemingly replacing Robert Parr, went back to Marrakech (1943), Casablanca (1944), Bordeaux (1944), Funchal, Madeira (1948), St Paul-Minneapolis (1950), Lourenço Marques, now Maputo (1953), concluding his career as Consul-General in Tangier (1957). He was appointed an OBE on 8 June 1944, a CBE on 1 January 1960[28] and died at Cleveland, Yorkshire, on 15 September 1978.

While serving in Casablanca and Marrakech, Bryce and Margaret Nairn became friends of Sir Winston and Lady Clementine Churchill. They met again, in July 1945, when both families were guests of Brigadier-General Brutinel[29] at the Chateau de Bordaberry, near Hendaye, France, close to the Spanish border. Here, Margaret Nairn is credited with encouraging Winston Churchill to take up painting again; the immediate result was his painting 'Villa on the Nivelle'.[30]

DR DIOT

Eric and Eileen called on Doctor Diot soon after their arrival. Eileen said he had been recommended by a friend of her brother, Laurence, in Paris.[31] Dr Diot said the climate was very good for lung complaints,[32] so ideal for Eric, although at that stage he had not really examined him but intended to. Eileen said that 'he wasn't particularly sympathetic, but he must be a good doctor and through him we'll be able to know that the chest is reacting properly'. He did advise that they must allow three-to-four weeks for 'acclimatisation' before expecting much.[33]

Dr Lucien Edmond Diot had served in Marrakech since 1929. He graduated from the University of Nancy in 1922 and studied at the Pasteur Institute in Paris, where he may have had contact with the friend of Eileen's brother. On 5 April 1929, Dr Diot became the head of the Regional Laboratory of Bacteriology, Medical Officer and the head of the Anti-Syphilitic Dispensary at the *l'Hopitâl Mauchamp*[34] (now *l'Hopitâl Ibn Zohr*[35]), Avenue Guemassa[36] in the city. The role of his laboratory was to help with the detection of disease and to prevent further transmission of communicable diseases through the isolation of patients. Although the hospital was just a nine-minute walk from where the Blairs subsequently stayed and close to the British Consulate, there is no further reference to Dr Diot in the correspondence of either Blair.

By January 1939 Eric reported that being in Morocco had done his lungs a good deal of good. He did not cough much now and had put on half a stone.[37] This rather cheerful self-assessment overlooked the continuous stomach upsets (from the water), bouts of cold and Eric's suffering from the extreme heat when they first arrived, all of which Eileen had reported in her correspondence. Eileen particularly suffered from 'upsets', possibly food-poisoning, but more probably from mosquitoes and the heat.

Dr Diot's son, Jacques (1925-2017), was to become a French war hero, serving with the Second Armoured Division, formed in Temara, Morocco, in August 1943, under General Philippe Leclerc;[38] his division landed at Normandy and was one of the first to enter Paris. Jacques was seriously injured in the fighting and convalesced in Morocco, presumably under the care of his father, before returning to France.[39] In 1946, he married Henriette Engel and they lived in St Martin d'Heres, near Grenoble, where he died in 2017.

Winston Churchill was a regular visitor to Marrakech, often staying at the Hotel Mamounia, where there is now a Churchill Suite. In January 1948, while holidaying and writing his memoirs, Dr Diot treated him for bronchitis. He prescribed M and B, a sulphonamide antibacterial medication, which Churchill had used before.[40] He recommended that Mr Churchill stay indoors because of his age – he was then 73 – and recent pneumonia and a weak heart.[41]

Churchill telegraphed his wife and Lord Moran, his personal physician, to say 'it was a bad cough in the tubes, but not in the lungs has now lasted for six days without temperature or improvement. Neither Dr Diot or I could say that condition is serious enough to warrant your journey here'. Later he asked Lord Moran to come saying 'at my age everyone has to be careful'.[42]

Churchill made a further visit in 1950 and recorded: 'I asked Dr Diot to come to see me in order to see how he was getting on. He has been frightfully ill and, after twenty-five years' hard service in Morocco, he has been removed to take charge of the laboratory. He says he has a highly competent successor to whom he is going to introduce me, in case I need him at any time.'[43] Dr Diot became responsible for the Laboratoire d'Analyses Médicales on Avenue du Guéliz, later Avenue Mohamed V, where he was still working in 1956, some six years after his second encounter with Churchill.

KEVIN CARTER

ABEL DÉSIRÉ BEZERT

Eric and Eileen signed a six-month lease to stay at Villa Simont, a contract arranged by Monsieur Abel Désiré Bezert, a former soldier who was born in 1873 in Mazan, a commune near Avignon in the Département of Vaucluse. He served with the 40th Infantry Regiment from 17 November 1894, but was injured when munitions exploded while serving in Bonifacio, Corsica in December 1895. From 1898 he lived between Montélimar and Bastia, but served several periods in prison for crimes including embezzlement and complicity, stealing oats, printing false money and opening a café without approval. He moved to (Ciudad) Bolivar in Venezuela in 1912.[44] He undertook auxiliary military service in Corsica in 1916, but was deemed free from military service in 1921, before finding his way to Marrakech.

He owned a shop, *Bezert Ameublement*, at 14 Avenue du Guéliz, (now Avenue Mohammed V), Guéliz, which among other things offered villas to rent.[45] The shop was taken over by a company called Fotis in December 1936. In December 1937, Bezert was seriously injured again when knocked from his bicycle by a car in Guéliz. He continued to ply his trade and helped the Blairs to find their villa. Eric signed a contract on 18 September 1938, and paid an advance rental of Frs 550 for the first month, from 15 October to 15 November.[46] The contract is signed by Bezert on behalf of the owner; he wrote Simont, rather than Simon,[47] and *propritair* rather than *propriétaire*.

CHEZ MADAME VELLAT

As Villa Simont was not available for another month, Eric and Eileen found accommodation at Chez Madame Maria Vellat. She was the widow of a French solicitor; her husband had died in December 1937.[48] The former office and house of Madame Vellat's late husband were at 12 Rue Edmond Doutté[49] (now Rue Moulay Ismail[50]), within the Médina, on the southern edge of Jemaa El Fna. Madame Vellat advertised rooms, with or without full board, in publications including *La Revue du Touring-club de France*.[51]

Madame Vellat was assisted by a cook-general, Aicha, who was paid Frs 6.50 per day (compared to the usual Frs 5 or sometimes 3.50 or even 3), but without food or lodging. Eric described Aicha as an extremely good plain cook who, in England, would be worth £50 a year (the equivalent of Frs 170 per week), and her keep.[52]

In a diary entry, Eric referred to the son of a Madame M. as being at St Cyr,[53] France's foremost military academy;[54] this was possibly the son of Madame Maria Vellat.

MÉDINA

Here, on the edge of the Jemaa El Fna, Eric and Eileen would have experienced all life: traditionally-dressed water-sellers, story-tellers, musicians, fire-eaters, acrobats and vendors of everything imaginable, much unimaginable. Exotic animals including snakes and their charmers, macaque monkeys and ostriches and within its labyrinthine bazaar, camels and donkeys,[55] with their owners calling 'bellak', imploring people to move out of the way.

Eric found 'mendicancy' so bad that it made it intolerable to walk through the streets and the poverty very severe, with people sleeping in the street. Blindness was common and many suffered from ringworm and deformities. Refugees camped outside the town from the famine districts further south.[56] The poverty in the Jewish quarter, which had a population of about 13,000, was even worse.[57] Writing about ghettoes in the Daily Mail in December 1938, Charles Graves (brother of poet and historical novelist Robert Graves) described the Jews in Marrakech as being 'packed as tight as sardines in appalling squalor'.[58]

Eileen found the native quarter (Médina) 'picturesque', but the smells only rivalled by the noises. She also found the European quarter (Guéliz) 'intolerable with a second-rate respectability and very expensive'.[59]

By 26 September, Eric had decided he did not care much for the country and was pining to be back in England, although this supposed there was no war there.[60] Two months later he still felt that 'on the whole this is rather a dull country'.[61] He compared the French colonial methods to his experience in Burma (and India), concluding that they were 'every bit as bad as us … economically it is just the usual swindle for which empires exist'. He drew some positives from the fact that there was a white proletariat, or near proletariat, so less of the white man's burden and less colour-prejudice.[62] He found that minor officials, for example officials at the post office, clerks and traffic policemen, were French, whereas in India they would be Indians.[63]

This was the first time Eric and Eileen had visited a country as tourists. Eric had less than no belief in theories about certain climates being 'good for' you – 'they always turn out to be a racket run by tourist agencies and local doctors'.[64] He was fatigued by the need to bargain with Arab shop-keepers who enjoyed the negotiation.

Eric and Eileen had planned to accommodate Eric's sister, Avril, but she chose not to travel, perhaps because of the unflattering descriptions given in the letters of her brother and sister-in-law. Eric's former commander from Spain, Georges Kopp, also considered the possibility, but did not visit, most likely because of financial constraints; he was accommodated by Eileen's brother and family in Greenwich, instead. Eileen also invited Geoffrey Gorer[65] to stay, if he was travelling to the south of Europe.[66]

They found it difficult to find an entrée into the Arab or other communities.[67] Attempts to contact socialist movements through the Independent Labour Party failed.[68]

They did know an (unnamed) educated Frenchwoman who wrote to *Maroc Matin* praising French Premier Daladier[69] and Eric discussed military deployments with Harold Maral, whose miltary service was with the Zouaves.[70]

Maral was a Licensed Professor of English, a teacher at the College de Marrakech, later at the Lycée Mangin and then the Lycée Victor Hugo (the International School), all in Marrakech. Married with two children, he lived on the Avenue Raymond Poincaré (later Haouz, now Avenue Hassan II), Guéliz. He was an active member of the Roman Catholic Church and also a follower of Robert Baden-Powell and ran the first Scouts de France troop in Marrakech from 1927 to at least 1937. Later, he retired to Rue Champlain, Tours, France.

The Blairs did not attend either the Catholic church (L'Église des Saints Martyrs which opened in 1928) or Protestant gatherings; at the time they met either at La Mairie – the Town Hall – or at the home of a member of the community. These may have provided introductions and invitations to coming festivities, although Eric considered that the French community hardly celebrated Christmas, only the New Year.

For the Blairs, Christmas came and went without particular note, other than the purchase and dispatch of presents to friends and family back in the UK. Eileen was ill with a cold on the day, which was passed subsequently to Eric, and they did not realise it was Christmas until the evening. They planned to eat a Christmas pudding, when it arrived, but they were still waiting on 26 December.[71] Eric did make notes of Yom Kippur (5 October 1938) and Ramadan, which began on 25 October 1938.

OTHER VISITORS TO MARRAKECH

Edward E. Long, CBE, a Fellow of the Royal Geographical Society, who visited at the same time, gave a much more enthusiastic account of Marrakech, saying that 'in these days it is certainly a marvel to find a city with a superb situation and outstanding climatic advantages which has retained a great deal of its native character and charm whilst offering the visitor first-class facilities'. He illustrated his article with a photograph of a villa in the European quarter (Guéliz, la Ville Nouvelle), supplied by the French Railways, the National Tourist Office and, with less consideration, a group of women shielding their faces from the camera in the vegetable market in the Médina.[72]

Vincent Korda, brother of film producer and director Alexander Korda, also visited Marrakech in December 1938, to understand colour and local costumes ahead of the Technicolor filming of the *Thief of Bagdad* (sic)[73], for which Vincent won an Academy Award for Best Art Direction in 1940.

A Mr C. Elliott, another December 1938 visitor to Marrakech, had an even more noteworthy experience at the time of the Blairs' stay, which he duly reported in a letter to the Editor of *The Times*, published on 7 December 1938, and which would have amused the Blairs if they had seen the cutting or met either of the protagonists.

> AN ARAB AND MR CHAMBERLAIN
>
> I was sitting at a cafe here the other day when an Arab boy of 13 came up to me and said in French: 'You are English, aren't you?' I was reading an English paper at the time. When I said 'Yes,' he said: 'You come from the land of Chamberlain. He is a good man. All of us Arabs love him, because he has given us peace' – a remark which I think ought to put to shame those of my fellow-countrymen who seem to have no word bad enough for Mr. Chamberlain, who has in the words of that little Arab boy, 'given us peace'.
>
> Mr C. ELLIOTT, Hotel Mamounia, Marrakech, Morocco.[74]

The Hôtel Mamounia on the Avenue Bab Djedid (Jdid), the same street as the British Consulate, was used by Thomas Cook for their visitors to Marrakech, by both rail and motor coach. This hotel, although not named by Eileen when describing the Majestic, was probably the most expensive in the city at the time.

Irene Hughes, a travel writer visiting Marrakech in January 1939, focused her comments on the African oral story-telling tradition and the performance of a 'prince of story-tellers', accompanied by tom-toms, in the Jemaa El Fna.[75]

Writer, art critic, old-Etonian, and sometime contributor to *Horizon*, Sacheverell Sitwell and his wife, Georgia (née Doble), visited Marrakech as part of a grand tour of the Maghreb, towards the end of the Blairs' stay, but there is no record of any meeting.[76] Sitwell wrote about their travels, including the visit to Marrakech, which he described as gay, a town of music, but also a place of dust and flies. He was taken with the history, architecture, gardens, food and people, in a way that evidently Eric and Eileen were not. The Sitwells' travels had, at least in part, been 'made possible' by the directors of the Compagnie des Chemins de Fer du Maroc.

Sitwell devoted a whole chapter to the Jemaa El Fna and another to Marrakech writing enthusiastically about the benefits of the military occupation, considering that the Morocco Protectorate 'may become the greatest achievement of the French Colonial Empire'.[77]

Nor did Eric make a record of the visit in mid-February 1939 of General Sir Edmund Ironside, the Governor of Gibraltar.[78] Eric wrote about him in his war-time diary on 12 February 1941, describing him as 'an old fool' and his decision to take the title Lord Ironside of Archangel, where he had fought the Bolsheviks in 1918, as 'an atrocious piece of impudence'.[79]

PHOTOGRAPHS

Eric and Eileen took two rolls of film while in Marrakech, now held by the Orwell Archive. As well as taking pictures of each other, they photographed Arab (or Berber) women and children, a group of three legionnaires and of a military bandsman playing at the Jenan (Jnane) el Harti[80] gardens in Guéliz, where they performed each Sunday afternoon. Perhaps this was also the public garden where Eric saw the gazelles (and looking at their hindquarters, thought of mint sauce).[81]

VILLA SIMONT

On 15 October, Eric and Eileen moved to Villa Simont, Sidahan,[82] Rue de Casa(blanca), Marrakech,[83] the main road north out of the city, about six kilometres from the Jemaa El Fna, but about a kilometre from the Bab Khemis or Bab Doukkala gates of the Médina. The road, since renamed the Avenue Mohamed Abdelkrime El Khatabi,[84] is now a dual-carriageway containing six-storey buildings along much of its length, as well as a university campus and the main railway station where the Blairs alighted and departed.

Villa Simont was owned by Boucher Simon, a well-known character at the Guéliz market. His full name was Simon Fankhauser, a Swiss-born member of the mainly French Protestant community in Marrakech. This group had links to British people in the city at the time, particularly through the South Morocco Mission; it may have been through this connection that the British Vice-Consul, Bryce Nairn, suggested Villa Simont to the Blairs.

The Fankhauser family then lived in a villa in the nearby street of Rue Verlet-Hanus[85] (now Rue Mohamed El Bequal[86]) in Guéliz. Son Ernest, also known as Simon, later owned a boucherie/charcuterie in Vidauban, in the Département of Var, near Marseilles. Granddaughters Marguerite, Rose-Marie and Elisabeth survive and still have connections in Marrakech.

Villa Simont was outside of the main built-up area of Marrakech – grand-daughter Elisabeth Fankhauser says it was *'près de la sixième borne kilometrique sur la route de Casablanca'* so close to the sixth kilometre stone and was surrounded by orange groves, part of a 'Park'.[87] With a few outbuildings, it was close to the Quartier Militaire and lay below the fortified hills immediately to the west of the town, where French guns commanded the Arab quarter[88] and on the road to the rifle range.

Both Eric and Eileen were uncertain about postal arrangements for the villa, so organised a *Boîte Postale* 48 at the post office in Guéliz.

The villa was slightly more expensive, but quieter to work in than Chez Madame Vellat. Eric also had the need for a bit of garden and a few animals – and space to fire his catapults, which had a range of 90 to 150 yards.[89]

By the beginning of November they already had a few flower seeds coming up, phloxes and sweet peas and things.[90] They had also sowed some nasturtiums, but these withered in the early morning frost. Eric had the rather pleasant experience of seeing the oranges and lemons on the trees frosted all over, but was unaffected by them.[91] The main crop had already started to ripen by the middle of October.[92] Eric wrote that Monsieur Simont used blood, in considerable quantities ('which he can get as he is a butcher') for manuring the orange trees.[93]

The house itself had a large sitting room, two bedrooms, a bathroom and a kitchen, and a kind of observatory for Eric to work in. Eric and Eileen furnished the house with grass and willow chairs, two rugs, a praying mat, several copper trays, a bed and several camel-hair couvertures, three whitewood tables, two charcoal braziers for cooking about a third of the essential crockery and some chessmen,[94] for about £10.[95] They lit fires, using wood (there was no coal), cooking on charcoal, and later a butane gas Primus stove.

As would have been customary for an expatriate home at the time, staff looked after the house and tended the animals, as well as the orange groves. Both Eric and Eileen mention Mahjroub (or Mahdjoub or Madhjub) Mahommed, who had spent between 10 and 12 (perhaps 15) years with the French soldiers and received a pension of Frs 5 a day.[96] Mahjroub also told them that there was 'going to be war' and that it was going to be the same as last time i.e. against Germany. Mahjroub had fought in the Great War and, although unable to read any language, had sufficient knowledge of geography to be aware that you had 'to cross the sea to get to Europe'.[97]

Mahjroub often called Eileen *Mon vieux Madame* and she wrote playfully about the conversations and work they shared. Mahjroub did the shopping, pumped the water and washed the floors while Eileen did the cooking and curiously enough the washing.[98] (Underwear was possibly an issue.)

Mahjroub also helped Eric to milk the two goats by holding their head and hind legs. Eric fed the goats, but noted that M. Simont's recently bought half-starved donkey would come over to rob the goats of their barley. Eric and Eileen bought twelve (soon reduced to eight) egg-laying chickens, along with two turtle-doves, who walked the house one behind the other. (The doves cost Frs 10, which Eric thought was over-expensive.)

Eric referred to M. as our servant and M(onsieur) (Simont)'s caretaker and discussed with him religious beliefs and practices, including during Ramadan.[99] [100] Eric noted that they appeared to be strict about not drinking, but that *kiff,* a type of cannabis, was widely-smoked. (Eric tried it without effect.) He later wrote that owing to poverty, they 'are not over scrupulous about what they eat'.[101]

Mahjroub cycled from the Médina to the house each morning arriving at around 7 am with fresh milk and bread. He departed after lunch although the initial arrangement had him staying until the evening, sleeping in the stable in the afternoon (especially during Ramadan); Eileen preferred him to go rather than stay just to wash up the supper things.[102]

At the beginning of December, Boucher Simon sacked Hussein, another of his employees at the villa, on the grounds that he was lazy. His role had been to tend two acres of orange and lemon trees and to look after a few sheep, for which he would have been paid about Frs 10 per day plus quarters. Eric said that Boucher Simon complained that Hussein was a Cleuh (C/Shleuh), so a Berber[103] from the south of Morocco. According to Eric, he evidently had some Negro blood too, although when Hussein's unnamed wife advised Eric that their brown goat was in kid, he referred to him as an Arab.[104] Eric noted that 'the Chleuh were regarded by Arabs as stupid, shiftless and avaricious; Europeans shared the prejudice too'.[105]

OUED TENSIFT

On 20 October, the Blairs visited the Oued Tensift, the area's principal river; its nearest point was about two kilometres to the north of the villa, further along the Rue de Casablanca. The river's source is high in the Atlas Mountains, near the Tizi-n-Tichka pass, the gateway to the Sahara and close to Taddert. It flows to Souira Guedima (Aguz), between Safi and Essaouira on the Atlantic Ocean.

When they visited first, the deep river bed was almost dry, but following considerable rain on 25 October – the first day of Ramadan – it was flooded feet deep and the land around had turned into marsh.[106] By 22 December, it had filled the whole of the valley it runs in, although it shrank to half the size the following day.

TADDERT

In a letter to Jack Common, Eric said that as soon as he had done the rough draft of his novel, *Coming Up For Air*, they were going to take a week off and go into the mountains, which at that time were covered in snow.[107] Eric said that the mountains appeared close, but were actually 50-100 miles away. Eric finished the draft by 13 January 1939 and Eric and Eileen travelled 95 kilometres to Taddert, which lies at about 1,650 metres in the High Atlas Mountains, an area with heavy snowfall in winter. The bus journey took three hours there and two-and-a-half back.

They stayed at the Auberge 'Les Noyers'[108] (the Walnut Inn), appropriately located in the middle of ancient walnut trees, which would have appealed to Eric. Monsieur Lequeux, *Propriétaire*, gained local notoriety when his wife 'disappeared' from the marital home in 1937. A few months later Lequeux was the driver of a Camionette Légère (light truck) which crashed on the road to Marrakech, four kilometres north of Taddert. A 25-year-old female passenger, who may have been seeking employment at his hotel, was killed in the accident.

The stationery of the Auberge[109] described the hotel as having comfortable rooms, running water and electricity, a café and a restaurant which offered meals at all hours. It described the hotel as being at a pleasant location at an altitude of 1,650 metres, from which Eric presumably took his measurement. Eric said it was like a cheap hotel in Paris and the cafés *en route* were similar too.

The (French) people they met were typical lower-middle class, living exactly the same life style, 'except that they are obliged to speak a little Arabic'.[110]

Here they found little Berber mountain villages of mud huts where they cultivated terraces in a style that reminded Eric of the hills of Burma. 'The kind (of Berbers) round here are the Chleuh.' What fascinated Eric was their white skin, with red cheeks, the beautiful eyes of the women – exceedingly striking – 'and most of all that they were so dirty'.[111] Sacheverell Sitwell was taken with their beauty too (and their dancing).[112]

In a conversation with friend Tosco Fyvel a few years later, Eric claimed he had become increasingly attracted to young Arab (Berber?) girls and with Eileen's agreement, slept with one, presumably during this trip. Even then Fyvel was not sure that this was true or imagined,[113] although Eric had a similar conversation – describing the bliss of certain Moroccan girls – with Harold Acton at the Hôtel Chatham in Paris in 1945.[114] It is hard to think, perhaps, how Eileen may have occupied herself if these encounters did, indeed, happen in this remote mountain town.

LEGIONNAIRES

While they were in Taddert, Eric met an unnamed German member of the Foreign Legion involved in an electrical installation. He had left Germany during the period of high unemployment and intended to serve his full time to earn a small pension and so avoid imprisonment for desertion from the German army. The Legionnaires were involved in many infrastructure projects and credited with building more than 3,000 miles of roads in Morocco, including the main route between Casablanca and Marrakech, where it was then possible to drive at speeds of up to 80 mph.[115]

At the time of Eric and Eileen's stay there were some 15,000 regular troops in Marrakech, except for officers and NCOs, all Arab or negro (Senegalese), and a detachment of the Foreign Legion who were looked on as dangerous ruffians.[116] (Eric later added that there were some white troops.) The Blairs would have been able to watch the troops moving in and out of the city from their villa on the main road to Casablanca and close to the Quartier Militaire (now *Caserne Youssef Ibn Tachfine*).[117]

Eric later said that in Marrakech they did not meet any Europeans, except when five soldiers from the Foreign Legion called to see them: Craig (Glasgow Irish, but Orange); Williams (an American who claimed to have seen the last lion shot in Morocco in 1924[118]); Rowlands (possibly Eurasian); Smith (an American); and an unnamed young Scot. All were still privates. There were two or three other English or Americans in this group, but 'Englishmen etc. don't get on, will not put up with the rough conditions etc. and are handicapped by their inability to learn the language, which the Germans were better able to do … so took the NCO roles'.[119]

In February 1939 – while the Blairs were still in Marrakech – two German Legionnaires, Benkardt and Schmidt, were executed by firing squad in Fez for the murder of one of their officers, Captain Prague of the Legion's Artillery, in Marrakech seven months earlier.[120] They declined to wear blindfolds.

RETURN TO ENGLAND

Eric and Eileen remained at Villa Simont until about 20 March 1939. The villa and the surrounding park were later sold to the Steel-

Maitland family[121], descendants of Sir Arthur Steel-Maitland (1876-1935), the first chairman of the Conservative Party. The last known owner, Lady Brenda Steel-Maitland, died in 2002, leaving most of her estate, including Castle Gogar (near Edinburgh Airport), to Mr Gordon Stewart, a school teacher, who was one of her tenants. According to reports, she spent her final years living in 'aristocratic decay' between the castle and her orange groves in Morocco.[122]

Eric's last diary entry in Marrakech, on 21 March 1939, was headed Hôtel des Négociants, which was located in the Avenue du Guéliz (now Avenue Mohamed V); they may have spent their final night there. The Négociants was – and remains – a popular café for the expatriate community and visitors.

On the previous day, Eric and Eileen had watched a visit to Guéliz by the Sultan of Morocco and noted that the Arabs had 'a great feeling of loyalty to him, in spite of his being under the thumb of the French'. Madame Vellat told Eric that the Arabs would even make a sign of obeisance when hearing the Sultan's voice over the radio.[123]

The Blairs spent a few days in Casablanca, before embarking on their return journey at 4pm on 26 March 1939, a little over six months after their arrival in Morocco. They travelled to London in the second of three classes at a cost of £6 10s on the Japanese ship, the 11,950 tons *MS Yasukuni Maru*,[124] landing on 30 March 1939.[125] On the manifest, Eric described himself as a writer, while Eileen stated that she was a housewife. They gave their address as 24 Crooms Hill, Greenwich, London SE10, the home of Eileen's brother, Laurence, and his wife.

As a merchant vessel, delivering tea among other things, the *MS Yasukuni Maru* carried only 65 passengers. (Eric counted just 25 in second and third classes, but the manifest lists more.) Among the passengers were Dora Philby (née Johnston), the mother of Kim Philby, and his then 18-year-old sister, Diana Mary. They sailed first class, so the Blairs probably were unaware that they were fellow-travellers.

They had boarded at Suez while travelling from Arabia – where husband St John had been an adviser to Ibn Saud, the first monarch and founder of Saudi Arabia – to their home in Hampstead. Three months later, on 20 July 1939, St John Philby fought the Hythe, Kent, by-election, representing the British People's Party. He lost his deposit.

GHOSTS OF ORWELL PAST

Madame Vellat, Monsieur Désiré Bezert and Boucher Simon all died within the next 15 years and are each laid to rest at the Cimetière

PAPER

Européen de Marrakech, on Rue Erraouda (Arrawda) in Guéliz. The cemetery, which opened in 1925, is well maintained with graves laid out in a grid system and has a memorial obelisk to the 333 French military servicemen buried there,[126] part of the Carré Militaire Français.

There are a number of German names among the memorials at the military cemetery. Arthur Williams, possibly the Legionnaire who visited Villa Simont, was buried at the Military Cemetery in Essaouira in 1942.

The registers and site plans of the cemetery, held in the small office by the front gates, show that Monsieur (Abel) Désiré Bezert died on 28 October 1944, aged 72, and is buried in grave number 440F which is inscribed, without accents, 'Ici Repose Abel Desire Bezert Decede Le 28 Octobre 1944 A L'Age de 71 Ans P.P.L.'

Madame Vellat was buried on 12 January 1947, aged 73, in an unmarked grave number 483F. Boucher Simon (Fankhauser) died on 3 March 1953, aged 61, and is buried in grave number 1011A (not 1011O as mis-recorded in a second register). The memorial reads, again without accents, 'Ici Repose Fankhauser Simon Decede Le 3-3-1953 A L'Age de 61 Ans'.[127]

The cemetery's mason, Gueney Mustapha, and caretaker, Abdul Latif, helped us to locate each of the graves and as marks of respect, kindly watered the two stone memorials and also the ground where Madame Vellat was laid to rest.

Alas, there is no later trace of Aicha or of Mahjroub Mahommed, who most likely sank, like Madame Vellat, back into the nameless mounds of the graveyard[128] or Hussein or his wife, below a patch of good grass, where cattle browse among the graves, in the High Atlas Mountains.[129] (Although I note here that wealthier Arabs and Berbers in Morocco do, indeed, have headstones, with names.)[130]

BOOKSHOP MEMORIES

Having laid some of the Blairs' contacts to rest, we went in search of a bookshop and found *Librairie et Papeterie Chatr* (sometimes Shatlr, and at the time of the Blairs' stay, bookseller Martin) at 21, Avenue Mohamed V, previously Avenue du Guéliz. We were delighted to find Bernard Crick's biography of Orwell on prominent display, particularly as this French edition has the photograph of Eric writing at Villa Simont on the front cover.[131]

The staff there had read the book and knew that Orwell once lived in Marrakech, but not that he had stayed within a few hundred metres of their shop. They found a copy of *Animal Farm* in unreadable (for me) Arabic to add to my collection of Orwell books.

Unusually for books in this part of the world, it has an outline of a pig on the cover. *Nineteen Eighty-Four* was available to order but, alas, time did not permit.

ACKNOWLEDGEMENTS

In the preparation of this article, I referred to Eric's diaries and Eric and Eileen's correspondence and to the essay 'Marrakech', relying on the remarkable work of Peter Davison and his twenty-volume *Complete Works* and the additional volume, *The Lost Orwell*, and also the Orwell Archive at University College London. I am especially grateful to Monsieur Michel de Mondenard and his blog *Mangin@Marrakech* which tells the story of the French diaspora in the city they know as *la Rouge* in the 20th century. After a brief inquiry about the whereabouts of Rue Edmond Doutté, he kindly identified the modern names of the roads of the French Protectorate mentioned in the Blairs' papers and found a number of references to the places the Blairs stayed and their contacts in the French – and Swiss – communities in Marrakech.

NOTES

[1] See Royal College of Surgeons: *Plarr's Lives of the Fellows*. Available online at https://livesonline.rcseng.ac.uk/client/en_GB/lives?_ga=2.106497995.992209841.1565341625-1361716912.1565341625, accessed on 9 August 2011

[2] Eileen's letter to Norah Myles, December 1938 (Davison 2006: 76)

[3] Eric's letter to Francis Westrope, 25 August 1938 (*CWGO*, 11: 190)

[4] Eric's letter to Jack Common, 25 August 1938 (*CWGO*, 11: 191)

[5] Two other essays on local conditions, written for the publication *Quarterly* have not been found, yet (*CWGO*, 11: 237)

[6] Morocco Notebook (*CWGO*, 11: 307-308)

[7] According to Eric's notebook, the cost of hiring a bicycle was overcharged at Frs 6 per day 'should be 4 or 5'

[8] *CWGO*, 12: 20-57; first published as part of *Inside the Whale and Other Essays*, 11 March 1940

[9] *SS Stratheden* was built by Vickers-Armstrong of Barrow, earlier in 1938. It was broken up at Spezia in 1969

[10] Eric's Morocco Diary, between 3 and 10 September 1938 (*CWGO*, 11: 268 and 269)

[11] Manufactured by Schering-Kahlbaum A. G. of Wedding, Berlin (since 2006, part of Bayer A. G.)

[12] Eric's letter to his French translator Yvonne Davet, 11 September 1938 (*CWGO*, 11: 195)

[13] Eileen's letter to Eric's mother, 15 September 1938 (*CWGO*, 11: 198)

[14] Eric's letter to Jack Common, 19 March 1939 (*CWGO*, 11: 345)

[15] Most often Jemaa El Fna is considered to be the Arabic for *gathering area* which seems apt, but there are a number of other possible translations, including *place of death*

[16] Eileen's letter to Eric's mother, 15 September 1938 (*CWGO*, 11: 198)

[17] Eileen's letter to Norah Myles, December 1938 (Davison 2006: 76)

KEVIN CARTER

[18] *Le Petit Marocain*, 17 September 1934

[19] Georges Clémenceau (1841-1929), French Prime Minister during World War One

[20] El-Mansour-Eddahbi (1549-1603), Sultan of Morocco (1578-1603)

[21] Ibid

[22] Mamounia is generally translated as *safe haven*. The hotel was the subject of a song, Mamunia, written by Paul and Linda McCartney after a stay in 1973

[23] Approximate exchange rate at his time was Frs 170 = £1

[24] Correspondence with Monsieur Michel de Mondenard (Mangin@Marrakech), February 2019

[25] Eric's Morocco Diary, 22 November 1938 (*CWGO*, 11: 232)

[26] Correspondence from Thomas Livingstone-Learmonth, April 2019

[27] *Daily Record*, 3 March 1945

[28] *Foreign Office Lists* (1937-1938 and 1963) London: HMSO. The Foreign and Commonwealth Office library is now part of the Foyle Special Collection at King's College, London

[29] Brigadier-General Raymond Brutinel (1882-1964) was a geologist, journalist, soldier, entrepreneur and a pioneer in the field of mechanised warfare during World War One

[30] *Daily Telegraph*, 18 April 2011

[31] Eileen's letter to Eric's mother, 15 September 1938 (*CWGO*, 11: 199)

[32] Eric's letter to Dr J. B. MacDougall, 18 September 1938 (*CWGO*, 11: 201)

[33] Eileen's letter to Eric's sister, Marjorie Dakin, 27 September 1938 (*CWGO*, 11: 207)

[34] The hospital was named originally after a Dr Mauchamp who was murdered in Marrakech in 1907, accused of spying for France. France used this as a pretext for moving troops into Casablanca

[35] Ibn Zuhr el-Iyadi (or Avenzoar) (1094-1162) was an Andalusian scholar

[36] Guemassa (Gmassa) is a town to the south west of Marrakech

[37] Eric's letter to Geoffrey Gorer, 20 January 1939 (*CWGO*, 11: 321)

[38] Philippe François Marie Leclerc de Hauteclocque, a French general during World War Two. He is known in France simply as le Maréchal Leclerc, or just Leclerc

[39] The forum of *La 2ème Division Blindée de Leclerc*

[40] *Mirror* (Perth, WA) 3 January 1948: 3

[41] *Western Morning News*, 3 January 1948: 3

[42] *The Times*, 5 January 1948: 4

[43] Gilbert, Sir Martin (1988: 389)

[44] Archives of the *Département* of Vaucluse

[45] *Le Petit Marocain*, 9 December 1935

[46] UCL Orwell Archive

[47] To avoid (further) confusion, I have favoured the spelling used by Bezert, Eric and Eileen, so Simont

[48] *Le Petit Marocain*, 12 October 1937

[49] Edmond Doutté (1867-1926) was a French Arabist and Berberologist, explorer and author of books on the Maghreb, including Merrâkech (1905)

[50] Moulay Ismail ibn Sharif (1645-1727), Sultan of Morocco 1672-1727

[51] *La Revue du Touring-club de France*, April 1934

[52] Eric's Morocco Diary, 9 October 1938 (*CWGO*, 11: 219)
[53] École spéciale militaire de Saint-Cyr, France's foremost military academy, is located in Coëtquidan in Guer, Morbihan, Brittany
[54] Eric's Morocco Diary, 28 March 1939, written on board *MS Yasukuni Maru* (*CWGO*, 11: 347)
[55] Eric's letter to Leonard Moore, 1 October 1938 (*CWGO*, 11: 214)
[56] Eric's Morocco Diary, 13 September 1938 (*CWGO*, 11: 197)
[57] Eric's Morocco Diary, 27 September 1938 (*CWGO*, 11: 209)
[58] *Daily Mail*, December 1938
[59] Eileen's letter to Eric's mother, 15 September 1938 (*CWGO*, 11: 198)
[60] Eric's letter to Jack Common, 26 September 1938 (*CWGO*, 11: 205)
[61] Eric's letter to John Sceats, 24 November 1938 (*CWGO*, 11: 237)
[62] Eric's letter to Charles Doran, 26 November 1938 (*CWGO*, 11: 238)
[63] Eric's Morocco Diary, 8 January 1939 (*CWGO*, 11: 314)
[64] Eric's letter to Cyril Connolly, 14 December 1938 (*CWGO*, 11: 253)
[65] Geoffrey Edgar Solomon Gorer (1905-1985) was an English anthropologist, author and a friend of Eric and Eileen, until their respective deaths
[66] Eileen's letter to Geoffrey Gorer, 4 October 1938 (*CWGO*, 11: 218)
[67] Eric's letter to Jack Common, 29 September 1938 (*CWGO*, 11: 211)
[68] Eric's letter to John Sceats, 24 November 1938 (*CWGO*, 11: 237)
[69] Eric's Morocco Diary, 9 October 1938 (*CWGO*, 11: 219)
[70] Zouaves – a French light infantry regiment, particularly in North Africa
[71] Eric's letter to Jack Common, 26 December 1938 (*CWGO*, 11: 260)
[72] *Illustrated London News*, 5 November 1938: 39
[73] *Drayton and West Middlesex Gazette*, 2 December 1938: 16
[74] *Times* 'Points from Letters', 7 December 1938: 10.
[75] *Dundee Evening Telegraph*, 9 January 1939: 3
[76] *Lancashire Evening Post*, 1 February 1939: 4
[77] Sitwell, Sacheverell (1951 [1940]: 25-61)
[78] *Birmingham Daily Gazette*, 13 February 1939: 1
[79] War Time Diary, 12 February 1941 (*CWGO*, 12: 387)
[80] One translation of Jenan el Harti is 'Garden of Paradise'
[81] Orwell's essay 'Marrakech' (*CWGO*, 11: 417)
[82] Sidahan is not immediately recognisable as a Moroccan place name; it may refer to an earlier owner of the villa and/or the surrounding land, Si Dahan or Sidi Dahan
[83] Eric's letter to Jack Common, 26 September 1938 (*CWGO*, 11: 204)
[84] Abd el-Krim (1882-1963), Moroccan political and military leader who fought against Spanish and French colonisation. Eric made a cutting of a story about the arrest of his brother (*Presse Mondiale*, 18 October 1938)
[85] Edmond Émile Verlet-Hanus (1874-1914), a French soldier, Chevalier (1902) et Officier (1914) de la Légion d'Honneur
[86] Origin of this street's name not known
[87] Elisabeth Fankhauser's description, April 2019
[88] Eric's Morocco Diary, 27 September 1938 (*CWGO*, 11: 208)
[89] Eric's Morocco Diary, 2 Dec 1938 (*CWGO*, 11: 286)
[90] Eric's letter to Jack Common, 2 November 1938 (*CWGO*, 11: .231)

91 Eric's letter to Jack Common, 26 December 1938 (*CWGO*, 11;.261)
92 Eric's Morocco Diary, 12 October 1938 (*CWGO*, 11: 277)
93 Orwell, George (2009) Eric's Morocco Diary, 9 March 1939: 128
94 Eileen's letter to Norah Myles, December 1938 (Davison 2006: 77)
95 Eileen's letter to Geoffrey Gorer, 4 October 1938 (*CWGO*, 11: 218)
96 Eric's Morocco Diary, 22 November 1938 (*CWGO*, 11: 233)
97 Eric's Morocco Diary, 21 March 1939 (*CWGO*, 11: 346)
98 Eileen's letter to Norah Myles, December 1938 (Davison 2006: 77)
99 Eric's Morocco Diary, 1 November 1938 (*CWGO*, 11: 230)
100 The first day of Ramadan 1357, began on Tuesday 25 October 1938, the day the Blairs visited Oued Tensift
101 Eric's letter to Jack Common, 26 December 1938 (*CWGO*, 11: 261)
102 Eileen's letter to Mary Common, 5 December 1938 (*CWGO*, 11: 248)
103 Since 2011 the Amazigh (Berber) language has become one of Morocco's two official languages along with Modern Standard Arabic. French is widely spoken, too
104 Eric's Morocco Diary, 16 October 1938 (*CWGO*, 11: 277)
105 Eric's Morocco Diary, 10 December 1938 (*CWGO*, 11: 252)
106 Eric's Morocco Diary, 20 and 25 October 1938 (*CWGO*, 11: 279 and 280)
107 Eric's letter to Jack Common, 26 December 1938 (*CWGO*, 11: 261)
108 According to an on-line travel blog written in 2008, a Hotel des Noyers still existed in Taddert, seemingly in much reduced circumstances. See https://www.travelblog.org/Photos/2228812
109 Eric used two sheets of the hotel's stationery – overwritten with his Guéliz PO Box number – to write to Geoffrey Gorer on 20 January 1939 (*CWGO*, 11: 322)
110 Eric's Morocco diary, 7 January 1939 (*CWGO*, 11: 324 and 327)
111 Eric's letter to Geoffrey Gorer, 20 January 1939 (*CWGO*, 11: 321)
112 Sitwell, Sacheverell (1951 [1940]: 60)
113 Fyvel, T. R. (1982: 109)
114 Acton, Harold (1971: 152 and 153)
115 *Northern Daily Mail*, 28 December 1938: 8
116 Eric's Morocco Diary, 27 September 1938 (*CWGO*, 11: 207)
117 Youssef Ibn Tachfine or Tashfin and variations (reigned c. 1061-1106) was leader of the Berber Moroccan Almoravid empire and one of the founders of city of Marrakech
118 Eric's Morocco Diary, 18 February 1939 (*CWGO*, 11: 426)
119 Eric's Morocco Diary, 12 March 1939 (*CWGO*, 11: 342 and 343)
120 *The Scotsman*, 22 February 1939: 12
121 In April 2019, Elisabeth Fankhauser referred to the sale of the Villa and 'Park' to Lady Steel Midland (sic)
122 *The Scotsman*, 3 March 2003
123 Eric's Morocco Diary, 21 March 1939 (*CWGO*, 11: 345 and 346)
124 *MS Yasukuni Maru* was built by Mitsubishi in Nagasaki in 1930 for the high-speed European service. Later, in 1939, it was used to evacuate Japanese diplomats and civilians from Germany and then as a troopship. It was destroyed by torpedoes from the submarine *USS Trigger* on 24 January 1944 off the coast of Truk in the Pacific

[125] Manifest for Nippon Yusen Kaisha Merchant Ship *Yasukuni Maru*, which sailed from Yokohama and arrived in London on 30 March 1939

[126] Website *Findagrave* available online at https://www.findagrave.com/cemetery/2510187/cimetière-europeen-de-marrakech has a list and photographs of most of the military, but not civilian, memorials

[127] Extracts from the two-volume hand-written alphabetical registers of the Cimetière Européen de Marrakech, Rue Erraouda, Guéliz

[128] Orwell's essay 'Marrakech' (*CWGO*, 11: 417)

[129] Eric's Morocco Diary, 27 January 1939 (*CWGO*, 11: 326)

[130] Eric's Morocco Diary, 8 January 1939 (*CWGO*, 11: 315)

[131] Crick, Bernard (2008)

REFERENCES

Acton, Harold (1971) *Memoirs of an Aesthete 1939-1969*, New York: Viking Press

Bennani, Mounia (2017) *Villes-Paysages du Maroc*, Paris: Carré

Crick, Bernard (2008) *George Orwell* (trans. by Carretero, Stéphanie and Joly, Frédéric) Paris: Flammarion

Davison, Peter (ed.) (2006) *The Lost Orwell*, London: Timewell Press

Fiedler, Klaus (2018) *Interdenominational Faith Missions in Africa*, Mzuzu, Malawi: Mzuni Press

Fyvel, T. R. (1983 [1982]) *George Orwell: A Personal Memoir*, London: Hutchinson Paperback

Gilbert, Sir Martin (1988) *Winston S Churchill: Never Despair 1945-1965*, London: Heinemann

Orwell, George (1998, 19 [1952]) Such, Such Were the Joys, *Complete Works of George Orwell (CWGO)*, Davison, Peter (ed.) London: Secker & Warburg pp 356-387

Orwell, George (2009) *Diaries*, Davison, Peter (ed.) London: Harvill Secker

Shelden, Michael (1991) *Orwell: The Authorised Biography*, London: Heinemann

Sitwell, Sacheverell (1951 [1940]) *Mauretania Warrior, Man and Woman*, London: Gerald Duckworth and Co., third impression

NOTE ON THE CONTRIBUTOR

Kevin Carter is a founding life member of the Orwell Society. A former member of Her Majesty's Diplomatic Service, he spent much of the last forty years living and working outside the UK, most recently in Vienna, Austria. In February 2019, Kevin and his wife Sandra visited Marrakech, where his favourite Orwell book, *Coming Up For Air*, was written.

Orwell's Aunt Nellie

DARCY MOORE

George Orwell, aka Eric Blair (1903-1950), died on 21 January 1950. His favourite aunt, Nellie Limouzin (1870-1950), passed away five months later in tragically sad circumstances. Despite what one biographer describes as 'the suppression' of Limouzin from Orwell's accounts of his own life, it is evident how profoundly she influenced and shaped her nephew's early literary and political experiences. Blair may never have travelled far down the path to becoming the writer Orwell without his Aunt Nellie's encouragement, support and literary contacts.

Keywords: Eric Arthur Blair, Orwell, Ellen Kate Limouzin, Elaine Limouzin, Aunt Nellie, E. K. L., Eugène Adam, Lanti, Paris, Esperanto

In 1936, when Orwell was newly married to Eileen O'Shaughnessy (1905-1945), 'Aunt Nellie' strained the relationship somewhat by staying in their tiny spare bedroom for months (Davison 2006: 64). Eileen wrote in a letter to a friend that it was 'dreadful' and when she finally departed it felt like 'all our troubles' were over (ibid). In fairness, Nellie often house-sat when the Blairs were elsewhere and had originally found this cottage in Wallington for the couple. More significantly, a precedent was set some years earlier when the young Eric Blair had stayed in Paris with Limouzin and her partner, the writer and radical Esperantist, Eugène Adam (Wadhams 1984: 41).

At that time, the 24-year-old Eric Blair was desperate to escape 'five boring years within the sound of bugles' serving in the Indian Imperial Police (Orwell 1998 12: 272). He departed Rangoon in mid-July 1927 aboard the *MV Shropshire* and alighted in Marseilles, probably making his way to Paris by train to visit Aunt Nellie, who lived in the twelfth arrondissement (Barthelmess 1975: 14-15; Crick 1992 [1980]: 174-175). It was here, over the next few years, that animated discussion about literature, communism and politics was to take place with his favourite relative and her comrades, or in Esperanto, 'kamaradoj' (Borsboom 1976: 142).

Blair was in no hurry to get home to see his parents after a five-year absence. This brief initial visit to France was the first time he had complete personal freedom from the strictures of family, school, college and an ill-chosen career as a police officer. Contextually, it appears that Nellie played a significant role in her nephew's momentous decision to quit his well-paid job and become a writer. Limouzin and Adam had lives as writers and revolutionaries that must have appealed to the young Blair's romantic nature (ibid). There is no indication that he had already decided to resign on sailing from Rangoon but later in his life he would write that:

> When I came home on leave in 1927 I was already half determined to throw up my job, and one sniff of English air decided me (Orwell 1998 [1937] 5: 137-138).

Orwell's resignation took effect on 1 January 1928. This decision was a terrible shock and embarrassment to his family, especially to his father. Even worse was his intention – although unpublished except for boyhood poems printed in a local newspaper and a few pieces in his college magazine – to become a writer. After a brief period in Southwold and then London, he returned to Paris where he spent the next eighteen months endeavouring to become that writer. Just before departing London, he changed his occupation from 'policeman' to 'journalist' on his passport (Bowker 2004 [2003]: 104).

Blair returned to 14 Avenue de Corbéra in the spring of 1928 with his suitcase and caught the lift to an 8th floor apartment with central heating where his two contacts, Limouzin and Adam, very quickly assisted in furthering his literary ambitions (Bannier 1947). Although Blair did not live with the couple for long, and argued with Adam, this was a crucial period of his intellectual development (Wadhams 1984: 42). Blair, more than a decade later when he had 'transformed' into 'Orwell', described the Paris he experienced in the late 1920s as swarming with 'artists, writers, students, dilettanti, sight-seers, debauchees and plain idlers as the world has probably never seen' (Orwell 1998 12: 86). Blair's introduction to the radical, bohemian atmosphere that permeated the French capital during *les Années folles* (the Crazy Years) via this unusual couple, writing furiously in Esperanto under assumed names in support of international revolution, must have been revelatory. Nellie published using her initials, E. K. L., while Adam had assumed the identity of L'anti, 'he who is against the system' (Schor 2016: 145). Orwell's experiences in the artistic and bohemian space Nellie had created with her French partner, in that cramped Parisian apartment (Borsboom 1976: 142; Markov 1999: 113) followed five years of policing in what he came to understand was a corrupt system and 'a racket':

> I hated the imperialism I was serving with a bitterness which I probably cannot make clear (Orwell 1998 [1937] 5: 134).

DARCY MOORE Orwell was introduced to established, radical editors and writers of the calibre of Henri Barbusse (1873-1935) who had written the most widely-read French novel of World War One, *Under Fire*, by fictionalising his experiences with a small squad of soldiers in the trenches (Barbusse 1916). Adam and Barbusse were founding members of the French Communist Party in 1920 (Garvía 2016: 122) and Barbusse, on the behest of Adam, had served as honorary president at the first Sennacieca Asocio Tutmonda (SAT) Esperanto Congress held in Prague during 1921 (Lins 2016: 171). They both desperately wanted to change the social, economic and political system which had led to the massacre of a generation in the trenches. Barbusse, as a favour to his comrades, Limouzin and Adam, was to publish 'La Censure en Angleterre', Blair's first-ever paid article on 6 October 1928 in *Monde*, the journal he had founded and edited (Orwell 1998: 148-149). If one reads that early article closely it is evident that Nellie's experiences of censorship on the London stage were invaluable to the fledgling writer.

WHO WAS NELLIE LIMOUZIN?

Nellie Limouzin, sister of Orwell's mother, Ida Mabel Blair (1875-1943), was known by many names during her lifetime. Official records show she was christened in Moulmein, Burma, as Ellen Kate Limouzin (although her surname was transcribed incorrectly and often misspelt). She was Helene Kate Limouzin-Adam at her death in London, aged 79 (Wandsworth 1950). Theatre programmes reveal her stage name was Elaine Limouzin (Rudd 1999: 84) and her nieces and nephews called her Aunt Nellie. Occasionally she was known as Hélène in Paris and wrote articles and letters in Esperanto using her initials, E. K. L. (SAT Archive). Eric and his first wife, Eileen O'Shaughnessy, named one of their goats 'Kate' after her (Bowker 2004 [2003]: 230). Mostly, she was just Nellie.

Nellie's and Ida's father, Francis 'Frank' Limouzin, was a shipwright, raconteur and businessman (ibid: 7). Born in France, his family had been in Burma since the 1820s where his father had established a thriving shipbuilding business on the river at Moulmein where there was good access to timber (ibid). Frank's second marriage, to Thérèse Catherine Halliley, just a few months after the tragic deaths of his wife and two young children, produced eight children who mostly did not remain in Burma but were educated in England (Brennan 2017: 2). As a result of the boat-building industry collapsing at the end of the century, Frank moved into the rice business, losing most of his money in the process (Bowker 2004 [2003]: 10). It is interesting to note that many of Nellie's male relatives, in both the Halliley and Limouzin families, were freemasons (Membership Registers). It is worth noting also that Eugène Adam always perceived Nellie, who possessed a French passport, as an aristocratic Englishwoman (Boorsboom 1976: 45).

Nellie and Ida were sisters with wildly different life trajectories. Ellen Limouzin is recorded as a 'scholar' at a boarding school in Surrey on the 1881 census when she was ten and by thirty is an 'actress', according to the 1901 census (Brennan 2017: 2-3). Nellie could have been described at different stages of her life as a feminist, suffragette, prisoner, socialist, communist, writer, editor, teacher, vaudevillian and Esperantist. She was always a radical but paradoxically, like Orwell, had some old-fashioned, quite conservative beliefs (Limouzin 1931). She remained unmarried until she was well into her sixties.

Ida married the 40-year-old Richard Blair on 15 June 1897 at Naini Tal, a popular hill station 345 km northeast of New Delhi, when she was 22 (*Times of India* 1897). Eric Arthur Blair, their second child, was born six years later in sight of the Himalaya Mountains at Motihari. In 1904, Ida left India for England with her two children while her husband continued his work as a Sub-Deputy Opium Agent until retirement in 1912. Ida was mildly bohemian and approved of the many causes her sister championed but was busy raising three children alone. Aunt Nellie was always a presence, from the earliest of days, in Eric's life (Blair 1905).

Nellie was a suffragette who actively participated in highly influential, headline-grabbing demonstrations at the Houses of Parliament and obstructing public transport by sitting on tram rails (Boorsboom 1976: 45). She was photographed with the Pankhurst sisters in London c. 1909 (Duby 2019) and was an active member of the militant Women's Social and Political Union formed in 1903 by Emmeline Pankhurst (*Votes for Women* 1909). She is described as an 'ex-prisoner' in an article published in the WSPU newspaper where it is noted that she 'kindly recited a small piece entitled *The Brawling Brotherhood* which was greatly appreciated' (ibid). Many suffragettes were incarcerated in Holloway Prison during this period using pseudonyms and are difficult to identify (Davies 2018). Dione Venables, a cousin of the Buddicom children who were childhood friends with Orwell (Buddicom 2006), remembers conversation about 'Auntie Nellie having been arrested and imprisoned *maybe* more than once' (email correspondence 2020). During this period, Nellie lived in a rented top-floor apartment at 195 Ladbroke Grove in Notting Hill with friends from at least 1908 (London Metropolitan Archives). It became a literary salon of sorts and she came to know H. G. Wells, G. K. Chesterton, Edith Nesbit and the 'Red Vicar of Thaxted', Conrad Noel (Bowker 2004 [2003]: 16). Nellie flirted with communism after the Russian Revolution, which is also when she began learning Esperanto (Markov 1999: 113).

Nellie's acting career spanned three decades. She was a member of the Pioneer Players who performed banned plays and explored feminist issues, including women's suffrage (Rudd 1999: 84). They

PAPER

popularised the German-born Hrotsvit (935-1002), considered to be the first female dramatist and significantly, a woman who spoke truth to power (Cockin 1998: 115). The group cleverly formed as a private society or club enabling their productions to avoid the system of censorship administered by the Lord Chamberlain. Nellie was a member of the Women's Freedom League which was closely affiliated with the Pioneer Players and enthusiastically opposed theatre censorship (Rudd 1999: 75). The WFL caimed to revolutionise the relationship between women and men. This is particularly interesting, considering the nature of Nellie's relationship with Adam and Orwell's open marriage with O'Shaughnessy (Bowker 2004 [2003]: xi). She was probably a member of the Actresses' Franchise League founded in 1908 to support the suffrage movement; members wrote and produced plays for that cause (Cockin 2017).

Nellie's stage name was Elaine Limouzin (Duby 2019). She appeared during late 1912 in *Three Women*, staged at the Chelsea Town Hall and directed by Edith Craig (1869-1947) who was well-known for plays that publicised the women's suffragette movement (see British Library a and b). Elaine also appeared in *The Disciple* at Wyndham's Theatre in June 1914 (Carson 1914: 170-171) and it is possible that Orwell, attending Eton at the time, would have been in the audience for her performance in *At Mrs Beam's* during 1920 at the Kingsway Theatre in Holborn (Wearing 2014: 81). It appears that Limouzin only ever had minor roles but knew a great deal about how London theatre worked and how to circumvent censorship. It is not surprising that Blair's first published work, 'La Censure en Angleterre', opens with a paragraph that sounds as if it were dictated by Aunt Nellie:

> In the theatre, each play, before it is staged, must be submitted for inspection by a censor nominated by the government, who can ban its performance or request alterations if he thinks it a danger to public morality. This censor is just like any other civil servant and is not selected for his literary talents. He has either forbidden or held up the production of half the significant modern plays which have been produced in England in the last fifty years. Ibsen's *Ghosts*, Brieux's *Damaged Goods*, George Bernard Shaw's *Mrs Warren's Profession* – all strictly, even painfully moral plays – were kept off the English stage for many years. By contrast ordinary, and frankly pornographic, reviews and musical comedies have only suffered the minimum of alterations (Orwell 1998 10: 117).

Like so many other cultural experiences, Orwell was introduced to musical-hall comedy by his vaudevillian aunt (Bowker 2004 [2003]: 60).

It is worth noting that Eric Blair's second article, 'A farthing newspaper', published in *G. K.'s Weekly* in late December, was commissioned with Nellie's support as G. K. Chesterton was another literary contact (ibid: 109). The short stories that were rejected when he was in Paris also carried a note from an agent who hand-wrote: 'Give my best regards to Miss Limouzin' on the typewritten letter (Orwell Archive).

Nellie, although spending more and more time on the continent with Eugène Adam at Esperanto conferences from 1923 rather than on the stage in London, maintained the lease at her Ladbroke Grove apartment she had shared with other female housemates for two decades, until April 1928 (Bowker 2004 [2003]: 105). She was now completely committed to both Adam and the Esperantist cause and lived in Paris, in the apartment they shared, for a decade, from early 1926 (Boorsboom 1976: 71).

ADAM/LANTI AND THE ESPERANTISTS

In 1887, Ludwik Zamenhof, employing the pseudonym Dr Esperanto, published *Unua Libro (First Book)* in what he called lingvo internacia, the international language (Garvía 2016: 68). By 1889, speakers started referring to it as Esperanto ('a hopeful person') which soon became the official name (Foster 1982: 53-54). Eugène Adam, a life-long autodidact, began learning this language with a Catholic priest during World War One when he was a stretcher-bearer and an ambulance driver (Boorsboom 1976: 15-17). His war experiences made Zamenhof's goal – to create a language that would foster world peace and international understanding – appealing to Adam who had a reputation for providing medical aid to German, not just French soldiers (Schor 2016: 143-144). By 1920 Adam, who had initially been attracted to anarchism in his youth, became a founding member of the French Communist Party but soon became disillusioned (Boorsboom 1976: 20). He had become a committed Esperantist but his fervent anti-nationalism, gestated during the war, led him to believe that nation states fundamentally disempowered working people (Schor 2016: 144).

Adam wanted Esperanto to become the shared language of all revolutionaries believing that national languages prevented international cooperation. To this end, he founded the Sennacieca Asocio Tutmonda (SAT) in 1921 (Boorsboom 1976: 24). Adam was a charismatic speaker, energetic and a skilful, prolific writer. He was also a brilliant publicist. In late 1921, a press release announcing the suicide of Eugène Adam, the editor of *Sennacieca Revuo*, was issued by none other than Adam himself. A new editor, it was announced, E. Lanti, was to take the helm. This transformation into Lanti was amazingly successful since not everyone realised it was a hoax and, mistakenly, a genuine obituary was published sadly reporting that:

E. Adam, editor of *Sennacieca Revuo*, killed himself in October 1921 (ibid: 25).

SAT grew rapidly under Lanti's leadership and was at its zenith, becoming the largest Esperanto organisation with 6,500 members in 1929 (Lins 2016: 172).

Nellie, who was already learning Esperanto, joined SAT shortly after its founding (Boorsboom 1976: 45). As one of 300 delegates (Albert Einstein was honorary president but not present), she met Lanti at the Third SAT Congress held in Kassel, Germany, in mid-August 1923 (ibid). Nellie spoke publicly at the conference agreeing with his political views and Lanti was impressed with her intellect; a unique partnership developed based not on romantic love, but friendship and intellectual companionship which they agreed could be terminated if either party wished (ibid: 71). Lanti had progressive views on the political role of women within SAT and wrote about the conference noting:

> …there were few women present at the Congress, and even fewer took part in our business meetings. Such a lack will need to be eliminated from our movement. We must encourage our female comrades. And instead of arguing whether 'a Frenchman' or 'a German' ought to be on the executive committee, perhaps it would be more to the point to elect one woman (Lanti 1923).

They attended other conferences together and were photographed in Vienna at the 1925 congress (Boorsboom 1976: 138-9). Later that year, Nellie wrote to Lanti requesting that they live together in Paris where she would assist with secretarial duties and editorial work on the SAT journal (ibid: 71). He agreed. From 17 February 1926, Lanti resided at 14 Avenue de Corbéra with Nellie (ibid). They eventually married in 1934 when Adam divorced his first wife (ibid: 142). The relationship ended permanently when Lanti left for a world-wide tour in 1936 never to return to France (ibid).

Nellie moved back to England and lived with the newly-married Blairs (Davison 2006: 64). In Eileen's correspondence, one can see that Esperantists were the source of some mirth: 'I think I may be doing what the Esperantists call sleeping on straw – and as they are Esperantists they mean sleeping on straw' (ibid: 68). Eileen likely felt compassion at first for Nellie as it became clear that Lanti had deserted her to travel overseas. The truth of the matter is that they always had a progressive marital arrangement that did not oblige either to remain for longer than they wanted or needed (Boorsboom 1976: 71). Eileen had her own traditional Anglican marriage vows re-written so that she did not have to 'obey' Eric (Davison 2006: 64).

In 1947, Lanti committed suicide in Mexico acknowledging in his last note that E. K. L. was his legal wife and heir (Boorsboom 1976: 177). Sadly, Nellie was never able to claim this inheritance, old age or widow's pension and increasingly experienced ill-health due to financial worries (Picarda 1950).

E. K. L., LANTI, ORWELL, PSEUDONYMS AND ESPERANTO

In 1927, there was scant evidence that Blair would ever transform into a successful writer let alone the omnipresent 'Orwell' of today. E. K. L. and Lanti played crucial roles in nurturing his development. Blair's own pseudonym emerged six years later when his first published book, *Down and Out in Paris and London*, appeared in bookstores during January 1933, the month Hitler became Chancellor of Germany (Orwell 1997 [1933]). This book was written from experiences in just the last ten weeks of Eric Blair's time in Paris (Crick 1992 [1980]: 187). There is no mention of the relative he could have stayed with or sought sustenance from any time he wished. Obviously, this would not have assisted the construction of his tale of poverty and dissolution, but generally it was rare for Orwell to mention his relatives, in any context, anywhere in his writing. Six months after this first book was published, Nellie was writing to her nephew asking about the 'likelihood' that he would return to Paris and requested he write to her about the books she mentioned in her 'last letter' (Orwell 1998 10: 314).

Nellie was always reliable, providing literary contacts, employment and money whenever Eric needed succour. She had a close and lively relationship with her nephew which opened up his ways of seeing the world and even when rejected, these ideas proved invaluable to his intellectual, political and literary development.

Adam and Blair reportedly disliked each other and they quarrelled but the Frenchman did assist his literary career at the behest of Limouzin, as did other Esperantists (Wadhams 1984: 42). These included Francis and Myfanwy Westrope who employed Blair on Nellie's suggestion at *Booklover's Corner* in Hampstead (Orwell 1998 10: 354). Most commentators see Esperanto as less of an influence on Newspeak, in *Nineteen Eighty-Four*, compared to other artificial languages, particularly Basic English developed by C. K. Ogden (Garvía 2016: 1; 149-150) but it certainly had a considerable impact on Orwell's thinking. During the Spanish civil war in 1937, when Blair volunteered to fight fascism, there were a considerable number of Esperantists in the ranks. Andrés Nin (1892-1937), who was the leader of the Workers' Party of Marxist Unification (POUM) militia that Orwell joined, was fluent in the language and Esperanto was employed in their official bulletins (Lins 2017: 140). Speaking Esperanto was viewed as essential by many anarchists during this period and widely used in newspapers, on radio stations and by the Catalan government to provide information to the International Brigades (Garvía 2016: 1).

DARCY MOORE The influence of Aunt Nellie and Eugène Adam on Orwell's political and literary development has often been under-estimated in the biographies. Jeffrey Meyers (2000) and Gordon Bowker (2003) are the best for understanding the impact of Paris, Limouzin and Adam on Orwell's intellectual development. The former sees Adam as important in shaping Orwell's non-communist, left-leaning politics as a democratic socialist and Meyers posits that the writer's Englishness was confirmed by these formative experiences in France. Bernard Crick, who wrote the first full biography of Orwell, sagely suggests that:

> ... the suppression of Aunt Nellie and Eugène Adam from all later accounts of Paris is that they were, if not full-blown cranks, certainly crankish. And when George Orwell emerged from Eric Blair he wore the clothes of common sense (Crick 1992 [1980]: 190).

Orwell's dislike of socialist *cranks* is well-known, and he famously wrote:

> One sometimes gets the impression that the mere words 'Socialism' and 'Communism' draw towards them with magnetic force every fruit-juice drinker, nudist, sandal-wearer, sex-maniac, Quaker, 'Nature Cure' quack, pacifist, and feminist in England (Orwell 1998 [1937] 5: 161).

It appears that having an aunt like Nellie helped frame Orwell's thinking and one suspects a dry sense of humour rather than vitriol pervades his commentary about the progressive intellectual types he met or became acquainted with as a direct result of her progressive social causes (and writing). For example, Blair must have discussed his aunt's article, published in Esperanto during June 1928, celebrating one of her intellectual heroes, the geographer, anarchist and freemason, Élisée Reclus, who died in 1905 (Limouzin 1928). Although Reclus's proclivity for fruit-juice is unknown, he advocated nature conservation and was a vegetarian opposed to meat-eating or cruelty to animals with eccentric, strongly-held views on what he felt were the considerable benefits of nudism (Clark 2004: 107).

Stephen Wadhams interviewed friends, family and acquaintances of Orwell for a Canadian radio programme to mark the coming of the year in which *Nineteen Eighty-Four* is set (Wadhams 1984). One of his producers conducted a telephone interview in French with Lucien Bannier (1893-1986), an important Esperantist who knew Orwell (Wadhams: email correspondence). Somehow, the name was recorded as 'Louis' Bannier and every Orwell scholar since has made the same error. Bannier was always important as he is a primary source, actually spending time with Nellie and Adam together and observing their relationship with Orwell. Bannier's eyewitness account of an argument between Orwell and Adam has Blair proclaiming 'the Soviet system was the definitive socialism' (Wadhams 1984: 42). No wonder they quarrelled. Adam was an experienced writer and activist well-versed in the realpolitik of the world. His visit to Russia in August 1922 helped confirm for him that this was not the kind of revolution he supported (Lins 2016: 174). Shortly before he died, Orwell wrote:

> I could never be disappointed by the Stalin regime, because I never expected any good to come of it. ... Of course, one develops and modifies one's views, but I have never fundamentally altered my attitude towards the Soviet regime since I first began to pay attention to it some time in the nineteen-twenties (Orwell 1998 18: 443).

Adam was almost certainly the modifier. He was also a good model, having changed his own mind about a range of issues, especially during the early-1920s.

Many of the significant themes in Orwell's life and writing are sown during this period in the late 1920s but language, writing, ideology and the drive to publish deserve more emphasis. His professional and ideological challenges were numerous. Orwell's association with radical journal editors led to state surveillance (Smith 2013: 113-114) and he witnessed the internecine squabbles of those on the left, particularly intellectuals, which did not benefit ordinary working people. In 1944, Orwell said:

> For sheer dirtiness of fighting the feuds between the inventors of various of the international languages would take some beating (Orwell 1998 16: 82).

Adam, above all, was a writer prepared to work hard at his craft. Like Orwell, writing came above everything else, including his relationships and health. His motto: 'The writer must strive to avoid effort by the reader' (without castrating his thought) resulted in an 'outstanding' prose style which is approvingly described as 'simple', 'accurate' and 'elegant' (Sutton 2008: 102). Orwell's famous dictum, 'Good prose is like a window pane', comes rapidly to mind (Orwell 1998 18: 320).

Adam and Orwell shared a respect for artisans who made things with their hands and a genuine love of woodworking (Sutton 2008: 103). Adam was skilled at designing and making *faux*-antique furniture (Schor 2016: 143). Orwell's level of expertise was more that of an enthusiastic amateur (Bowker 2004 [2003]: 357). They were both self-deprecating and capable of ironic laughter whilst ostensibly to many eyes, austere and dour. Both despaired at 'the system' and were good at recognising the challenge of living a decent life in a corrupt society. Gordon Comstock, in Orwell's *Keep* the Aspidistra Flying, sees what Adam effectively lived his life trying to change:

> The mistake you make, don't you see, is in thinking one can live in a corrupt society without being corrupt oneself. After all, what do you achieve by refusing to make money? You're trying to behave as though one could stand right outside our economic system. But one can't. One's got to change the system, or one changes nothing (Orwell 1998 [1936] 4 : 235-236).

For Eugène Adam, like Henri Barbusse and Lucien Bannier, the horror of World War One led to a lifelong commitment to build a different system. The challenge, as Orwell knew only too well from his experience of imperialism in Burma and the corruption of an ideal witnessed during the Spanish civil war, was one of telling the truth.

Emphasis is often placed on Eric Blair's failure to make his mark as a writer during his time in Paris or to establish his career resulting in his retreat to the family home at Southwold by Christmas 1929. This is a misreading of the crucial importance of this eighteen-month period in Orwell's development. Perhaps this judgment was reached because no fiction was published; Orwell burnt two novel manuscripts and had all his short stories rejected by editors (Orwell 1998 10: 114). During this period Orwell's resilience was strengthened, and he remained determined to make a career as a writer, as it turns out, largely informed and framed by these experiences in Paris. His secretiveness, poor health and, most of all, ceaseless toil writing and seeking publishers for his work became a way of life until his premature death in 1950. Most importantly of all, Orwell learned to change his mind and admit he was wrong, a rare trait in a human being, especially a writer.

THE END

Only one letter (3 June 1933) written by Nellie to Orwell has survived (Orwell 1998 10: 314). It provides a fascinating intellectual and literary insight into her relationship with her nephew. Nellie mentions she is reading Machiavelli and Adrienne Sahuqué's Les Dogmes Sexuels, commenting that it is 'a refutation of the generally accepted ideas on sex as regards the contrast between the male and female and is based on biology ... the authoress is a serious scientist' (ibid: 314). The letter includes money, plus a subscription to a journal. Nellie wonders if there's 'any likelihood of your being able to come to Paris'. It is a tantalising glimpse into the intellectual world aunt and nephew shared and one senses there must have been many letters exchanged that are now lost. Paradoxically, Nellie wrote to Sennaciulo exactly two years before this letter complaining about having to 'read about the dirty habits of some African native' and that 'civilised people do have toilets, with keys, so in our literature we should also lock the door and thus prevent others from reading dirty, uninteresting details that may make our journal mockable' (Limouzin 1931). Nellie, born in 1870, held some beliefs and values, like her nephew's views on homosexuality, that have not aged well.

A letter that appears to be unknown to Orwell scholars, from the SAT Archive, reveals the ongoing assistance Nellie provided to Orwell's literary career (literally when he was on his deathbed). In early December 1949, she wrote to her Esperantist friend, Lucien Bannier, concerned that her 'Eriko' was too unwell to make the trip to Switzerland with his new wife (Limouzin 1949). Orwell was intending to convalesce at a Swiss sanatorium in a last-ditch attempt to treat the pulmonary tuberculosis which threatened his life. What is particularly interesting about this letter is that Nellie, unlike many of Orwell's friends and family, wholeheartedly approved of the 'very intelligent' Sonia Brownell as 'certainly a most suitable companion for Eric' (ibid). Undoubtedly, Nellie would have met Sonia at the hospital in University College London where Orwell was eventually to die. She goes on to explain that his latest novel, *1984*, has not yet been published in French but mentions it will be soon and asks for assistance in advertising it with 'serious bookshops'. Nellie reminds Bannier: 'His pen-name is George Orwell' (ibid).

Bannier had been assisting Nellie, unsuccessfully since Lanti's suicide, with matters pertaining to her husband's estate (SAT Archive). Nellie had not been re-united with Lanti since 1936 and he had often spoken cruelly about her to others suggesting she had no character, was soft and without backbone or willpower (Wadhams 1984: 42). He rarely wrote but there is one copy of a letter from Lanti to Bannier, in 1941, expressing dismay that he had not heard from E. K. L. and worried she had been killed during the Blitz in London by the Luftwaffe (Lanti 1941).

Another letter by Nellie written to Bannier on 17 April 1950, just a few months after attending her nephew's funeral, describes the penury and poor health she was experiencing as well as her travails with the French government regarding a disallowed pension:

> I am suffering from a persistent pain in my stomach and that weakens me to the point where I am inclined simply to crawl into bed … I believe that my poor health is partly the result of the frequent agitation of my nerves (and of my anger!) on account of the endless waiting for my much-needed money. Some time ago, I realised that I had nowhere near enough to pay the rent (the cost of electricity almost doubled in a year and I only use it for heating). So, I wrote to the French Consulate here to seek an allowance. But … could a 'child of the nation'

receive that? Absolutely not. The consul, instead of helping me, transferred me to some charity, completely made up of private individuals, I believe, and now instead of my own money, which French government bodies perpetually keep from me, I must accept a kind of charitable grant from an association of private people! They kindly send me an amount every two weeks and I have to accept it gratefully, when I could perfectly well extricate myself from the situation if only the government bodies did what they should. When I relate the whole story to English people, they either don't believe me or ask: 'Why not do this or that?' The very things which I had done from the start!! Here, once one has reached seventy years of age (or widows, I believe, immediately on becoming widowed), one can without any trouble receive at any post office approximately seventy pounds a year as a right. It is a pity for me that my father was indubitably French, or I could 'take back' British nationality, as two of my female acquaintances have done (Limouzin 1950).

Sadly, Nellie attempted suicide by opening the veins in her wrists shortly after this letter was written (Picarda 1950). Letters to Bannier, from a solicitor, explain that she suffered a nervous breakdown due to financial worries and was committed to Springfield (Mental) Hospital where she died, as recorded on her death certificate, on 22 June from a 'haemorrhage into a malignant glioma of the brain' (Wandsworth 1950). It is notable Nellie is recorded as being the widow of a 'French Professor of Languages' on this certificate (ibid). The solicitor described his surprise that Nellie had died, as he had visited a few days before and she seemed weakened but well enough (Picarda 1950).

There is no record of a cremation, burial plot or memorial at Wandsworth Cemetery or Putney Vale Crematorium, close to the hospital where she died. Her niece, Orwell's sister Avril Blair, was named as her heir. Only one newspaper reported her death (Duby 2019):

> Adam, Nellie (née Limouzin), aunt of Eric Arthur Blair (George Orwell).

- Special thanks to Vinko Markovo for his intellectual generosity in sharing archival material and David Lilley for his hard work translating documents written in Esperanto.

REFERENCES

Bannier, Lucien, *Letters*, SAT Archive

Barbusse, Henri (1916) *Le Feu: Journal d'une Escouade* [*Under Fire: Journal of a Squad*] Paris: Éditions Flammarion

Bartelmess, Norbert (1975) *Mia Vivo*, Paris: SAT

Blair, Ida (1905) *Diary*, Orwell Archive

Borsboom, E. (1976) *Vivo de Lanti*, Paris: SAT

Bowker, Gordon (2004 [2003]) *George Orwell*, London: Abacus

Brennan, Michael G. (2017) *George Orwell and Religion*, London: Bloomsbury Academic

British Library (a) Archive of Ellen Terry and Edith Craig, Loan MS 125/07/6, D178, Programme: *Three Women,* 13 November 1912

British Library (b) Archive of Ellen Terry and Edith Craig, Loan MS 125/07/6, D177, Programme Fragment: *Three Women,* 15 November 1912

Buddicom, Jacintha (2006 [1974]) *Eric and Us*, Finlay Publishers, postscript edition

Carson, Lionel (1914) *The Stage Year Book*, London: Carson & Comerford

Clark, John P. and Martin, Camille (eds) (2004) *Anarchy, Geography, Modernity: The Radical Social Thought of Elisée Reclus*. Lanham, MD: Lexington Books

Cockin, Katharine (1998) *Edith Craig, 1869-1947, Dramatic Lives*, London: Cassell

Cockin, Katharine (2001) *Women and Theatre in the Age of Suffrage: The Pioneer Players, 1911-1925*, London: Palgrave Macmillan

Cockin, Katharine (2017) *Edith Craig and Theatres of Art*, London: Bloomsbury Methuen Drama

Crick, Bernard (1992 [1980]) *George Orwell: A Life*, Harmondsworth, Middlesex: Penguin, second edition

Davies, Caitlin (2018) *Bad Girls: A History of Rebels and Renegades*, London: John Murray, Kindle Edition

Duby, Peter (2019) Elaine Limouzin, *Theatricalia.com*. Available online at https://theatricalia.com/person/jfs/elaine-limouzin, accessed on 17 January 2020

Forster, Peter G. (1982) *The Esperanto Movement*, The Netherlands: Mouton Publishers

Garvía, Roberto (2015) *Esperanto and Its Rivals: The Struggle for an International Language*, Philadelphia: University of Pennsylvania Press

Lanti, Eugène (1923) IIIa Kongreso de Sennacieca Asocio Tutmonda, Cassel, 11-15 aŭgusto 1923 [The Congress of SAT, Kassel, 11-15 August 1923], *Sennacieca Revuo*, Paris: SAT

Lanti, Eugène, (1940) *Leteroj de E. Lanti* [Letters of E. Lanti], edited by Varingjen, G., Paris: Sennacieca Asocio Tutmonda

Lanti, Eugène, *Letters*, SAT Archive

Lanti, E. (1970) *Manifesto de la Sennaciistoj* [*Manifesto of the Non-Nationalists*], Paris: SAT

Library and Museum of Freemasonry; London, England; Freemasonry Membership Registers; Description: Register of Admissions: Country and Foreign 'H', #736-939

Limouzin, Nellie (1928) Elisée Reclus, *Sennacieca Revuo*, 14 June 1928, Paris: SAT

Limouzin, Nellie (1931) El Sennaciulo, 11 June, Paris: SAT

Limouzin, Nellie (1949) Letter: E.K.L. to Lucien Bannier, 5 December 1949, Paris: SAT Archive

Limouzin, Nellie (1949) Letter: E. K. L. to Lucien Bannier, 17 April 1950, Paris: SAT Archive

Limouzin-Adam, Helene K. (1950) *Certified Copy of Death Certificate for Helene Kate. Limouzin-Adam,* 22 June, Wandsworth Register Office, UK.

DARCY MOORE

Lins, Ulrich (2016) *Dangerous Language: Esperanto under Hitler and Stalin*, London: Palgrave Macmillan

London Metropolitan Archives, London, England; Electoral Registers

Markov, Anne-Sophie (1999) *Le Mouvement International des Travailleurs Espérantistes 1918-1939* [*The International Movement of Esperantist Workers*], Université de Versailles/Saint Quentin-en-Yvelines

Meyers, Jeffrey (2000) *Orwell: Wintry Conscience of a Generation*, New York: W. W. Norton & Co.

Meyers, Jeffrey (2010) *Orwell: Life and Art*, Champaign: University of Illinois Press

Orwell, George (1998) *The Complete Works of George Orwell (20 volumes)*, Davison, Peter (ed.) London: Secker & Warburg

Orwell, George (2006) *The Lost Orwell: Being a Supplement to the Complete Works of George Orwell*, Davison, Peter (ed.) London: Timewell Press

Picarda, P. A. (1950) Letter to Lucien Bannier, 12 July, Paris: SAT Archive

Rudd, Jill and Gough, Val (eds) (1999) *Charlotte Perkins Gilman: Optimist Reformer*, University of Iowa Press

Schor, Esther (2016) *Bridge of Words: Esperanto and the Dream of a Universal Language*, New York: Metropolitan Books

Shelden, Michael (1991) *Orwell: The Authorised Biography*, London: Heinemann

Smith, James (2013) *British Writers and MI5 Surveillance, 1930-1960*, Cambridge: Cambridge University Press

Stansky, Peter and Abrahams, William (1972) *The Unknown Orwell*, New York: Alfred A. Knopf

Sutton, Geoffrey H. (2008) *Concise Encyclopedia of the Original Literature of Esperanto, 1887-2007*, New York: Mondial

Times of India (1897) Domestic occurrences, 22 June

Venables, Dione (2020) Email correspondence, 2020

Votes for Women (1909) Local notes, 25 June

Wadhams, Stephen (1984) *Remembering Orwell*, Harmondsworth, Middlesex: Penguin

Wadhams, Stephen (2019) Email correspondence

Wearing, J. P. (2014) *The London Stage 1920-1929: A Calendar of Productions, Performers, and Personnel*, London: Rowman & Littlefield Publishers

NOTE ON THE CONTRIBUTOR

Darcy Moore is a deputy principal at a secondary school in New South Wales. He teaches English and History and has worked as an academic in post-graduate teacher education at the University of Wollongong. His interest in Orwell began at school, thirty-seven years ago, when he was enthralled by *Animal Farm* and *Nineteen Eighty-Four*. He is currently working on a book, *Orwell in Paris*. He blogs at darcymoore.net and his Twitter handle is @Darcy1968. His Orwell collection can be accessed at darcymoore.net/orwell-collection/.

PAPER

Orwellian or Campbellian? 'Invisible Sources' in Orwell's 'Shooting an Elephant' and *Burmese Days*

CAROL BIEDERSTADT

While much has been written about the literary sources that influenced George Orwell's novels Animal Farm *and* Nineteen Eighty-Four, *little attention has been given to texts that may have influenced some of Orwell's earlier works. This paper examines the resemblance which Orwell's* Burmese Days *and his essay 'Shooting an Elephant' bear to several fictional and non-fictional works published before the release of his 1934 novel and 1936 essay. The author sets forth a case to suggest that the works of Reginald Campbell, a writer little known today but popular in the 1920s and 1930s, may have served as 'invisible sources' for Orwell's later texts.*

Keywords: George Orwell, Reginald Campbell, 'Shooting an Elephant', *Burmese Days*, 'invisible sources'

INTRODUCTION

Given the key words 'elephant', 'musth', 'mahout', and 'Orwell' from a 1930s narrative, most people would immediately think of George Orwell's 1936 essay 'Shooting an Elephant'. One of Orwell's most celebrated works, 'Shooting an Elephant', is one of three essays tied for fourth place in Literary Hub's list of 'The Most Anthologised Essays of the Last 25 Years', and several Google search results for 'the best English essays of all time' also feature the essay (see, for example, Allen 2013 and Reyzer 2016). Certainly, few would dispute the impact this essay has had on the world of literature. Many, however, would be surprised to know that the text from which the aforementioned key words were taken was not, in fact, Orwell's 'Shooting an Elephant' but Reginald Campbell's 1935 memoir *Teak Wallah*, published a year before the Orwell essay. The themes and wording of Orwell's essay bear a striking resemblance to those found in *Teak Wallah*. Yet the similarities between the works of Orwell and Campbell do not end there. Major themes of Orwell's *Burmese Days* (1989 [1934]) mirror in significant and indisputable ways those found in several of Campbell's early novels and shorter

CAROL BIEDERSTADT

works published as long as nine years before Orwell's 1934 novel. Is it possible to explain these similarities away as sheer coincidence – the result of two men having similar experiences while serving in colonial Burma and neighbouring Siam – or does the uncanny resemblance of these texts suggest that Orwell's essay and novel may have been directly influenced by the works of Campbell?

'SHOOTING AN ELEPHANT': FICTION, MEMOIR OR AUTOBIOGRAPHY?

The genre of Orwell's essay 'Shooting an Elephant' (1982 [1936] a) has been the subject of much debate with the authenticity of its detail widely disputed. Maung Htin Aung (1970: 27) and Stephen Ingle (1993: 11), for example, accept the essay as autobiographical, and Richard Rees also seems to view it as such (1962: 28). D. C. R. A. Goonetilleke, on the other hand, says it is 'doubtful whether [the essay] is fact or fiction', even though it is 'universally lauded as autobiographical' (1982: 182-183). Peter Davison, however, believes that Orwell did, indeed, shoot an elephant, citing as evidence the 'tape-recorded reminiscences of one of Orwell's colleagues in Burma, George Stuart'. Stuart, Davison points out, disputes only minor details, saying that Orwell killed the elephant in a single shot, not after multiple shots and a long, drawn-out period of suffering as depicted in the essay (1996: 46). In an explanatory footnote to Orwell's essay, Davison also points out Stuart's claim that Orwell was transferred to Katha, the town after which the fictitious town of Kyauktada in *Burmese Days* is modelled, as a consequence of having shot an elephant (1998: 506).

More recently, drawing on some of Orwell's poetry and the autobiography of Captain H. R. Robinson, a retired Burma Police captain, Gerry Abbott has provided yet another argument to suggest that Orwell actually shot an elephant (2016: 116-122). Lending even more support to this view, the narrator of *Burmese Days* describes a conversation between Flory and Elizabeth, saying: 'She was quite thrilled when he described the murder of an elephant which he had perpetrated some years earlier' (Orwell 1989 [1934]: 87). The repeated theme as well as the peculiar choice of the word 'murder' in describing the incident, the nuance of which echoes the sentiment expressed in the essay, are especially compelling. It is also possible that the essay's essential 'truth' lies primarily in the sincerity of the emotion it so convincingly conveys. As John Rodden suggests: 'Orwell may have used creative imagination in the essay, and it may best be described as what is now known as '"creative nonfiction"'. Still, Rodden says, the essay appears 'to be firmly rooted in fact' (2014: 31). For many of these reasons, I, too, have long argued that the essay is at the very least semi-autobiographical. Some recent findings, however, have left me questioning my earlier assumption.

REGINALD CAMPBELL: A 'FAMOUS AUTHOR'[1] LIKE ORWELL?

Nine years Orwell's senior, the young Reginald Wilfrid Campbell, born Reginald Wilfrid Wilder (according to the London, England, Church of England Register of Births and Baptisms) in Brentford, Middlesex, on 22 September 1894, seems to have had little in common with the young Eric Blair. Information about Campbell's early life is scant, but his father, Percy Wilder, does not appear to have been a part of his life for long, since the 1901 Census indicates that at age six, Campbell's relation to the head of the household in which he lived with his mother was that of 'visitor'. His 1927 marriage certificate lists his father as deceased (London, England, Church of England Register of Marriages and Banns), although exactly when he died is unknown. His mother, Selina Elizabeth Gosselin, whose name is indicated as Selina Campbell in the 1901 Census, died in 1903 when Campbell was eight. How Campbell spent the intervening years is not clear, but the 1911 Census shows that at age 16, he was a boarding student at the Berkhamsted School in Hertfordshire.

Campbell later served in the Royal Navy from 1912-1919 (National Archives) before signing on to work for the Anglo-Siam Company and boarding a steamship for Siam in May of 1919, about three years before Orwell went to Burma. Both the 1921 and 1924 editions of the *Directory for Bangkok and Siam* concur with Campbell's memoir, listing his occupation as 'Forest Assistant' (1921: 184 and 1924: 252). Company records, however, indicate that his employment agreement was 'terminated on the grounds of ill health' in late March 1924 (*Directors' Minute Book:* 97) and, in an April 1926 article, Campbell states that he 'returned to England from abroad a little over a year ago' ('My Literary Career': 5). If Campbell left Siam in 1925, he did so two years before Orwell left Burma. While of different backgrounds, then, the two men had at least one salient similarity: they served contemporaneously in the same region of Asia for about three years.

After a five-year stint in Siam – again paralleling Orwell's five years in Burma – Campbell returned to England and took up a career in writing. In a 1926 issue of the *New Leader*, a socialist publication that also featured several of Orwell's articles and reviews,[2] Campbell describes the stimulus for this new métier: his travels in the 'Near and Far East', he says, had provided him with 'material for a writer'. Lacking the practical know-how of the professional writer, however, Campbell recounts reluctantly enrolling, at the urging of a friend, in a correspondence course offered by Gordon Meggy's Premier School of Journalism. The decision appears to have been worthwhile, for under the mentorship of Meggy, Campbell achieved a degree of success; he claims that within twelve months, he had sold 80 per cent of the fiction he had written (ibid: 5), and evidence suggests that Campbell was, indeed, widely read. A 1934

CAROL BIEDERSTADT

issue of the *Cheltenham Chronicle and Gloucestershire Graphic*, for example, includes the uppercase heading 'COMPLETE STORY BY A FAMOUS AUTHOR' above Campbell's 'Timber-Working Elephants in the Siamese Jungle' (p. 3), and his novels were translated into six languages, including French, German and Spanish (*worldcat.org*).

THE INFLUENCE OF CAMPBELL'S MUSTHING ELEPHANTS: POSSIBLE OR PROBABLE?

My own interest in the works of Campbell began when I happened upon a copy of his memoir, *Teak Wallah*, in which he describes his experiences working with the timber elephants of Siam. He recounts an incident involving an elephant in musth (a period in which the bull is highly aggressive and experiencing a large rise in reproductive hormones). And while the episode concludes differently from the one described in Orwell's 'Shooting an Elephant', the two narratives bear many striking similarities. To begin with, both accounts are set in the early 1920s, Campbell's in Siam and Orwell's in Burma. In both cases, the men in charge – a heroic senior teak wallah in Campbell's account and the narrator in Orwell's essay – receive word that a tame elephant has gone musth and is running amok. Campbell's teak wallah sets out to investigate on a 'grey mare' (1935: 150), while Orwell's narrator sets out on a pony (1982 [1968]: 266). Other similarities in theme and language are perhaps best considered when viewed side by side:

Campbell's *Teak Wallah* (1935)	Orwell's 'Shooting an Elephant' (1936)
'Poo Kam Sen **went on "musth,"** and unfortunately broke the chain by which he had been secured to a tree, and got free' (op cit: 149).	'It was not, of course, a wild elephant, but a tame one which had gone "must". It had been chained up as tame elephants always are when their attack of "must"[3] is due, but on the previous night it had broken its chain and escaped' (op cit: 266-267).
'…the chief who owns the animal **is probably ten days' journey away,** and he, [Campbell's teak wallah], must be responsible for the safety of the village and its inhabitants' (op cit: 150).	'Its mahout, the only person who could manage it when it was in that state…**was now twelve hours' journey away…**' (op cit: 267).

'Two bullock-carts appear ahead. **The drivers just have time to flee,** and he is on them, **smashing the carts to matchwood** and **killing the patient bullocks**' (op cit: 150).	'It had already destroyed somebody's bamboo hut, **killed a cow** and raided some fruit-stalls and devoured the stock; also it had met the municipal rubbish van, and, when the **driver jumped out and took to his heels, had turned the van over and inflicted violence upon it**' (op cit: 267).
'**A Lao husbandman**, walking alone on the road. He hears a faint sound, the slur of the broken chain, behind him, and casually looks round. A scream of horror rises to his throat, strangles as a mountain surges upon him. **He is knocked down, crushed, and left a shapeless mass of flesh and blood on the road**' (op cit: 149-150).	'I rounded the hut and saw a man's dead body sprawling in the mud. He was an Indian, **a black Dravidian coolie**, almost naked, and he could not have been dead many minutes. The people said that the elephant had come suddenly upon him round the corner of the hut, caught him with its trunk, put its foot on his back, and ground him into the earth. …The friction of the great beast's foot had stripped the skin from his back as neatly as one skins a rabbit' (op cit: 267-268).
Earlier in the narrative, when the heroic teak wallah sets out to shoot a python: 'We began walking up the path, the mahout following behind on foot and a **mob of curious coolies trailing out behind him**' (op cit: 77).	'As I started forward **practically the whole population of the quarter flocked out of the houses and followed me**' (op cit: 268).
Campbell's teak wallah 'is **a man who loves elephants and would not willingly take the life** of one' (op cit: 152).	'As soon as I saw the elephant I knew with perfect certainty that I ought not to shoot him' (op cit: 268).
	'Moreover, I **did not in the least want to shoot him**' (ibid: 269).
	'But **I did not want to shoot the elephant**. … It seemed to me that it would be murder to shoot him' (ibid: 270).

CAROL BIEDERSTADT

The accounts differ somewhat at this point, for Campbell's teak wallah, unwilling to shoot the beast, digs a pit trap for it instead. Despite the differences in detail, however, the shared themes are unmistakable; of key importance, both texts reflect the loneliness endured by the white man in a position of responsibility over the 'yellow', including the fear of looking foolish and the rage induced by the mockery of the 'natives'. Both also mention the legality of shooting elephants, although in Orwell's essay, the reference feels inauthentic – an afterthought given as justification for the narrator's actions – whereas Campbell's teak wallah, knowing the animal 'can and should be shot', still seeks a humane resolution to the problem. Consider the following:

Campbell's *Teak Wallah* (1935)	Orwell's 'Shooting an Elephant' (1936)
Speaking of his dog: 'the thought struck me **that he was every bit as lonely as I, being one little "white" dog amidst a host of yellow pariahs**' (op cit: 125).	'Here was I, **the white man with his gun,** standing in front of the unarmed native crowd — seemingly the leading actor of the piece; but **in reality I was only an absurd puppet pushed to and fro by the will of those yellow faces behind**' (op cit: 269).
	But even then I was not thinking particularly of my own skin, only of the **watchful yellow faces behind**' (ibid: 270).
On being robbed: 'The news of the loss of the [cash] box would by now be all over the place, and in my imagination I felt that **everyone was laughing at me**. In the cold rage that soon enveloped me **I could have burned that village to the ground**' (op cit: 124).	'**The crowd would laugh at me**. And my whole life, **every white man's life in the East, was one long struggle not to be laughed at**' (op cit: 270).
On falling off a horse: '...the whole village turning out in the hopes of seeing me fall off a second time' (ibid: 51).	'...with another part I thought that the greatest joy in the world would be to drive a bayonet into a Buddhist priest's guts' (ibid: 266).
'...**the law of Siam being that rogues can and should be shot at sight, he should** suffer that fate before any more men are killed or property is damaged' (op cit: 152).	'Besides, **legally I had done the right thing, for a mad elephant has to be killed,** like a mad dog, if its owner fails to control it' (op cit: 272).

While not a key element in either, the concept of locals consuming elephant meat is also repeated in both texts. In *Teak Wallah*, Campbell describes becoming 'furiously angry' upon learning that a group of mahouts and chainmen had eaten a dead baby elephant. He explains: 'I suppose it is no worse to eat baby elephant than it is to eat veal but we dealt with elephants so much, and thought of them so highly, that the act seemed almost to savour of cannibalism.' Adding to his rage is the suspicion 'that the men had slain the little creature on purpose to eat it' (op cit: 273-274). While again differing in detail, the topic reappears in Orwell's essay; early in the account his narrator establishes that the Burmans 'wanted the meat' (op cit: 268), and he returns to the theme with a thinly veiled disgust – comparable to Campbell's furious anger – at the end of the narrative: 'Burmans were arriving with dahs and baskets even before I left, and I was told they had stripped his body almost to the bones by the afternoon' (ibid: 272).

It is, of course, entirely possible that the similarities above are sheer coincidence; there were, certainly, other reports of elephants escaping, 'breaking their fetters and occasionally killing their human riders in the process', in Siam and Burma (Saha 2017: 177). Hugh Nisbet, for one, describes a similar incident in which Mounggyi, a tusker in musth, breaks free and kills a man in Burma, and Nisbet even describes capturing the elephant using a pit trap similar to the one used by Campbell's teak wallah (1935: 19-22). Were the passages above the only parallels between Orwell and Campbell, it would be easy to dismiss them as coincidence; however, they are not the only prominent similarities.

Certainly the oddest and most perplexing similarity between 'Shooting an Elephant' and *Teak Wallah* involves a correspondence of an entirely different type. As he does with other figures mentioned in the memoir, Campbell conceals the actual identity of the heroic teak wallah. It has been suggested he was the well-respected Forest Manager of the Anglo-Siam Company, W. A. Elder (Travers-Murison 2019), although convincing evidence provided by Kittichai Wattananikorn suggests he was, in fact, Harry L. Norman, a Forest Assistant senior to Campbell (2019 and 2018: 159, 162). Regardless of the true identity of this individual, however, it is curious that Campbell chose to assign the heroic figure the fictitious name 'Orwell'. Thus, in Campbell's memoir, it is actually 'Orwell' who hears about the rogue elephant and 'foams in to the compound on his grey mare', 'Orwell' who, since 'the chief who owns the animal is … ten days' journey away … must be responsible for the safety of the village and its inhabitants' (op cit: 150), and 'Orwell' who 'is a man who loves elephants and would not willingly take the life of one' (ibid: 152). Can this curious choice of pseudonym, too, be attributed to nothing more than extraordinary coincidence?[4]

PAPER

CAROL BIEDERSTADT

At this point it is important to note that *Teak Wallah* is not the only one of Campbell's texts to focus on musthing elephants. Encounters with rogue or musthing elephants, for example, are described in many of Campbell's early narratives, including *Brown Wife – Or White?* (1925), 'The Mankiller' (1928), *Poo Lorn of the Elephants*[5] (1930a), 'The Humbling of Ai Poy and Ai Soo' (1930b), and *Jungle Night* (1935). All of these texts contain passages that Orwell's later essay conspicuously parallels in theme or language. For example, Campbell's 1925 novel, *Brown Wife – Or White?*, written ten years before the memoir, describes an elephant named Poo Ngurn that breaks its chains and runs amok while in musth. A villager tells the teak wallah: 'I saw with my own eyes an overturned bullock cart, the bullocks dead, the drivers … ' before completing the thought with 'an expressive flattening motion with outspread brown hands'[6] (p. 149). Once again, legal justification for shooting the beast is given: 'for the law in Siam allows wild elephants to be shot provided they are causing damage to life or property' (ibid: 86). However, this teak wallah, too, is unwilling to shoot the tusker, for in addition to his respect for elephants (he gazes at the threatening elephant with a 'look that amounted almost to reverence' [ibid: 85]), he is aware of the animal's monetary value: 'remember, no shooting if it can be avoided … Because he's our most valuable tusker, and is worth ten thousand ticals if he's worth a satang' (ibid: 150-151). This reasoning is also mirrored in Orwell's essay: 'It is a serious matter to shoot a working elephant – it is comparable to destroying a huge and costly piece of machinery – and obviously one ought not to do it if it can possibly be avoided' (op cit: 268-269). Likewise, in 'The Humbling of Ai Poy and Ai Soo'[7] (1930b), rafting assistant Mannering is notified about an elephant that 'engaged in lunching off the sweetmeats and rice-cakes on the market-stalls, and when these were finished … began demolition work', resulting in 'hut after hut [dissolving] into thin air', behaviour similar to that exhibited by the elephant in Orwell's narrative (op cit: 264).

While similar in that Orwell's essay and almost all of Campbell's early works explore the notion of 'shooting an elephant', however, it is significant that they do so in different ways. Orwell's narrator, like Campbell's teak wallahs, contemplates the position of the elephant's brain; unaware 'that in shooting an elephant one should shoot to cut an imaginary bar running from ear-hole to ear-hole', though, he aims 'several inches in front of this, thinking the brain would be further forward' (op cit: 271). His inappropriate weapon, a theme also explored by Campbell,[8] as well as his poor aim, lead to the brutal and drawn-out slaying of the elephant, a key theme in Orwell's essay. Campbell's teak wallahs, in contrast, never take such wanton actions. The teak wallahs of Campbell's *Elephant King*, for example, proud of never having 'laid one of these great animals low in the dust', do not 'even know the vital shot to the brain that is necessary to kill an elephant outright' (1930: 200). And in his other works, even those who know how to shoot an elephant properly and have legitimate reason for doing so still rarely shoot. Campbell's Mannering, for instance, while 'loath to shoot such a magnificent creature', runs his eye 'along the barrel and on to the thick root of the trunk that hides the brain' of Poo Oo, for he 'had now become unmanageable' and, thus, 'must pay with his life'. Fortunately for Poo Oo, another elephant bursts onto the scene, interrupting Mannering's actions (op cit: XVIII). In *Jungle Night,* an elephant trader, planning to shoot a killer he believes has been attacking his own herd, knows well the exact position for the 'vital shot to the brain' (1933: 244) yet never takes the shot. When he later learns that the real killer is his own Poo Taw, an elephant that 'meant perhaps more to [him] than a dog does to his master' (ibid: 12), he reluctantly commits to shooting him: 'One well-aimed shot at close range, and the whole thing would be over and done with. No suffering, no knowledge even of who had killed him, provided that the aim *was* true, which it must be.' Ultimately, though, he is unable to muster the courage to shoot his beloved Poo Taw and curses himself for 'a coward' and 'a weak-kneed fool' (ibid: 266-267).

Even in the rare case that one of Campbell's teak wallahs actually *does* shoot an elephant, it is only for good reason. In *Brown Wife – Or White?*, for example, Poo Ngurn, experiencing blood-lust after being goaded and shot at by a lout, is killed only to prevent the death of a woman he charges (ibid: 254). Likewise, in *Tiger Valley,* an elephant that has been badly mauled by a tiger is euthanised by gunshot 'as a last resort' (1931: 167), but it is a humane death: 'I shot at her at point-blank range, and she fell without a sound' (ibid: 169). A teak wallah in *This Animal Is Dangerous* faces a similar situation: '… he was a man, be it noted, who loved elephants, and the slaying of one, even to put it out of misery, was a hard thing for him to do' (1934a: 56). Clearly, 'man vs. rogue elephant' was a long-running and oft-repeated theme in Campbell's works, and the likelihood that Orwell encountered it in one of its variants is great. In actually shooting the elephant, however, Orwell's narrator takes a path not taken by any of the characters of Campbell's narratives.

THE PLOT THICKENS: SHADOWS OF CAMPBELL IN ORWELL'S *BURMESE DAYS*
Significantly, the similarities between the works of Campbell and Orwell do not end with 'Shooting an Elephant'. Campbell's first two novels, *Brown Wife – Or White?* (1925) and *Uneasy Virtue* (1926b), contain plot devices and themes that are not only reproduced in Orwell's *Burmese Days* but are also central to the storyline. Both of Campbell's early novels, for instance, feature teak workers who 'purchase' native wives or 'mistresses' who are later dismissed and replaced with white *memsahibs.* The shunned native women, with the help of sinisterly unscrupulous native men, then attempt to

CAROL BIEDERSTADT

bribe their former 'Lords', just as Ma Hla May, of *Burmese Days*, unceremoniously dismissed by Flory, bribes her former *'thakin'* at the prompting of the cunning U Po Kyin. The disgust of the memsahib upon learning her man has been sexually intimate with a local woman, a pivotal point in Orwell's novel, is also found in Campbell's first novel. Consider the similarities:

Campbell's *Brown Wife – Or White?* (1925)	Campbell's *Uneasy Virtue* (1926)	Orwell's *Burmese Days* (1934)
'**Chan Som**. She would have to be told, of course, that he was bringing out a **mem-sahib** next year, and the sooner he broke the news to her after his arrival at Muang Ngon the better it would be for both him and her, **but it was going to be a painful business…**' (op cit: 33).	'"The Master sent for me?" she inquired. "Yes. **Me Dee, I am bringing a mem-sahib up here**," he said slowly. "Wooi," she exclaimed. "Soon?" "Yes. Almost directly." "**Then I go?" "You go"**' (op cit: 50).	'Meanwhile, Flory **had turned Ma Hla May out of his house. A nasty, dirty job!** There was a sufficient pretext … but still, it was only a pretext. Flory knew perfectly well, and Ma Hla May knew, and all the servants knew, that he was getting rid of her because of Elizabeth. Because of "the Ingaleikma with dyed hair", as Ma Hla May called her' (op cit: 116).
Kitty comes across a photo of 'a pretty brown girl and a tiny baby, and the baby's eyes were strangely blue for a native's, they were reminiscent … **a wave of horror suddenly flooded Kitty Denton's whole being, and for the first time in her life she crumpled up on the hard teak floor in a dead faint…**' (op cit: 165).		'Elizabeth glanced across the aisle at him, and **her revulsion made her almost physically sick. … The thought that he had been the lover of that grey-faced, maniacal creature made her shudder in her bones**' (op cit: 286).

'Blackmail, by Gad! At the thought an uneasy feeling made itself manifest in the pit of his trembling stomach, then stilled as with a breath of relief he remembered that **Mrs. Denton could speak but little of the Lao language, while the girl now before him knew not one word of the English tongue**' (op cit: 195). Me Ooan: '"What I would tell her is that the Lord Denton kept a girl of my race, by whom he had a son. I would mention that they are even now in the village. I have proof." Anderson swayed and nearly fell; here was **blackmail** with a vengeance' (ibid: 196).	'"I want one thousand ticals, Master. … If you do not give me the money, I will tell the mem-sahib of something. … **I will tell her that you have kept me. I cannot speak her language, but I have proof**"' (op cit: 214).	Flory 'thought Ma Hla May quite capable of coming back and making a scene. Not that it mattered much, **for neither girl knew a word of the other's language**' (op cit: 89). 'It was from Ma Hla May – or rather, it had been written for her and she had signed it with a cross – and it demanded fifty rupees, in a vaguely menacing manner. … he reflected that the tone of the letter was curious, for **he had not expected Ma Hla May to begin blackmailing him so soon**…' (ibid: 132).
Me Ooan: **'I want money…'** (op cit: 194).	Me Dee: '"I want at least one thousand," she told him. "According to the custom"' (op cit: 51).	Ma Hla May: *'Pike-san pay like! Pike-san pay-like!'* ('Give me money! Give me money!') (op cit: 284)
'"**Were you not my husband?**" she replied. "I have a right to money, much money, since **you sent me away for no fault of my own and gave me nothing in return**"' (op cit: 194).		'"How can I go back… **I who have been a *bo-kadaw*, a white man's wife**… Two years I was your wife, you loved me and cared for me, and then without warning, without reason, you drove me from your door like a dog"' (op cit: 158).

PAPER

CAROL
BIEDERSTADT

'"Look here, I will give you two hundred ticals, which is all I have. I could give you a little more later, perhaps..."' (op cit: 197).		'"I will give you money. You shall have the fifty rupees you asked me for – more later. I have no more till next month"' (op cit: 159).

Furthermore, the scene in *Burmese Days* in which the British Club is besieged by a Burmese mob after the odious Ellis blinds a young Burman by hitting him with a stick[9] is also reminiscent of a scene in Campbell's *Uneasy Virtue*, despite the more convoluted plot of the latter. Wanting higher pay and angered that an Englishman had abandoned his relative, Me Dee, for a white wife, the cunning head raftsman, Nai Pliang, convinces the local teak rafters to strike. When their demands are not met, Pliang refuses to salaam to the arrogant Saunders, the man who had spurned Me Dee. Saunders responds by cursing him in the foulest possible language and dealing 'the Lao a smashing blow on the chest which sent the man sprawling' (op cit: 105). Saunders is then shot at with an arrow, and after taking refuge in his home, he and his British peers are besieged by an angry mob. Unable to call for the gendarmes, they remain trapped in the house until a respected teak wallah from a neighbouring forest eventually saves them (ibid: 107-110), just as Flory eventually saves the day in Orwell's novel. These parallels, however, are only the most significant similarities between *Burmese Days* and Campbell's earlier works; the stories explore numerous other similar themes, including the loneliness and isolation of the British teak worker, the avarice and cunning of native women, and English spinsters who come to the colonies and British-held areas in search of husbands.

The striking similarities between *Burmese Days* and Campbell's earlier novels raise a series of questions that may actually shed light on Campbell's curious decision to name the heroic teak wallah in his 1935 memoir 'Orwell'. First, is it possible that Orwell borrowed some of the themes of *Burmese Days* from Campbell? And in turn, could Campbell have read Orwell's novel and recognised that his own themes and storylines had been appropriated – and improved upon – by the young George Orwell? Might this, perhaps, have caused Campbell to christen his heroic teak wallah 'Orwell', a sort of 'insider joke'? In turn, might seeing his own name in a narrative about a man faced with the prospect of having to shoot an elephant against his will have triggered any ideas for Orwell?

ORWELL AND CAMPBELL: TWO SHIPS IN THE NIGHT?

While I have not located evidence that definitively connects Orwell and Campbell, it seems likely that Eric Blair, an avid reader with an interest in the themes on which Campbell wrote, had read some of

Campbell's works. Even in Burma, Campbell's novels would almost certainly have been available in Orwell's favourite bookstore, Smart and Mookerdum's.[10] As noted by Bernard Crick, 'each P. & O. liner brought the latest books and even literary periodicals from England' to the bookshop (1982 [1980] 157), and Campbell's shorter works were widely published in periodicals including the *Illustrated London News, Everybody's Magazine, Munsey's,* the *Popular Magazine, Pearson's* and *Romance*. Similarly, his novels were widely reviewed and discussed in publications including the *Sketch,* the *Illustrated London News* and numerous local papers.[11] Some of his longer works were also serialised,[12] while some of his shorter works were anthologised.[13] With so prolific an author writing about themes so close to Orwell's own interests, it seems highly unlikely that an avid reader like Orwell would never have encountered any of Campbell's works.

It is also significant that Orwell makes Flory, the protagonist of *Burmese Days,* a timber merchant. As I have argued elsewhere, Flory was a semi-autobiographical representation of Orwell himself, and in depicting him as a timber merchant Orwell was able to avoid creating an obvious *roman-à-clef* (2019: 13). The timber merchant, of course, was a natural choice for the young Orwell as it was a familiar occupation; his maternal relatives in Moulmein had, after all, been in the ship-building and timber trade 'almost from the time that port city had been ceded to the British in 1826' (Stansky and Abrahams 1972: 11). In fact, Limouzin & Co. was founded by Orwell's maternal great grandfather, G. E. Limouzin (Langham-Carter 1947: 50), and the family was so renowned in Moulmein that a street was named after them[14] (Larkin 2005: 183). Furthermore, his uncle, Henry Branson Ward, husband of his aunt Nora Grace Limouzin, had served as a Burma Forestry Service worker (1911 England Census).

It is, thus, likely that Orwell encountered some British forestry workers and teak merchants through family connections while posted in Moulmein, and he may even have heard of the exploits of the heroic teak wallah Campbell describes. It is also conceivable that Orwell and Campbell crossed paths at some point as the Ngao forest station where Campbell worked is less than 300 kilometers from Moulmein. Moreover, Moulmein was well-known to teak workers in Siam. As Kittichai Wattananikorn (2018) points out, before the Chiang Mai Treaty of 1874, amended in 1883, and the royal edict of 1884 on the trading of teak, wherein the British came to effectively monopolise teak-felling in Siam, many of the men working the Siamese forests had been Burmese, Mon and Shan, all British subjects (ibid: 23-24). Indeed, Moulmein had been 'a more popular destination than Bangkok for the Burmese merchants, the Haw Chinese from Yunnan, and even for the British' (ibid: 9). The Bombay Burmah Company also had an office in Moulmein, from which it sent its men to the Lanna region through well-established routes (Wattananikorn 2019). While this sort of travel would have been less common in the 1920s, it was not unheard of; indeed, several of Campbell's stories, including 'Prestige', describe people crossing to and from Burma on foot (1928a: 125). Likewise, in *Brown Wife – Or White?*, a teak wallah says that the best route from England to the Siamese forests is 'via Rangoon and Moulmein and then across country to Siam', explaining that this 'is a much quicker way than by going all the long sea journey round Singapore and Bangkok, and then coming up-country from the latter place partly by rail and partly by path through the jungle' (op cit: 187). Finally, not only does Campbell mention Burma in several of his stories, he even sets some of them in Burma. His short story 'Just to Add Interest' (1927), for example, describes an incident involving two men 'in joint charge of a great teak forest in central Burma' (ibid: 159). While based in Siam, then, it is clear that Campbell was no stranger to Burma.

CONCLUSION: THE 'INVISIBLE SOURCES' BEHIND ORWELL'S BURMA NARRATIVES

No writer lives or works in a vacuum, and George Orwell certainly did not. It is well known that the works of writers such as Yevgeny Zamyatin and H. G. Wells, for example, influenced Orwell's dystopian masterpiece *Nineteen Eighty-Four*. Yet as Jonathan Rose points out, also important were the works of writers such as Olaf Stapledon and Alfred Noyes – unacknowledged influences Rose refers to as 'invisible sources' because 'Orwell never mentioned them in his writings' (1992: 132-136). I suggest that Reginald Campbell's works, too, were likely 'invisible sources' that inspired Orwell's novel *Burmese Days* and his essay 'Shooting an Elephant'. *Burmese Days,* of course, differs in plot from Campbell's works, yet it still clearly mirrors Campbell's earlier writings in its key aspects of theme, character, conflict and wording. Likewise, 'Shooting an Elephant' echoes Campbell's 'rogue elephant' narratives in all of these key aspects, yet its resolution markedly differs from any written by Campbell – Orwell's cowardly narrator shoots and kills the elephant, after all – something the teak wallahs of Campbell's narratives would never have done, certainly not simply to save face before a crowd of 'natives'.[15] Campbell makes this clear, in fact, in a scene in *Elephant King* when a conference of men assembled to kill a rogue elephant ultimately refuse to take action; the narrator explains: 'A queer ending … but these men dwelt in a country where elephants are valued for their lives instead of their deaths' (op cit: 173). But perhaps this crucial difference brings us closer to a possible solution to the mysterious connection between Orwell and Campbell, for unlike Campbell, Orwell was not a teak wallah, and his political purpose in writing his essay as well as his intended audience differed dramatically from those of any of Campbell's narratives.

Replying to a query from John Lehmann, editor of *New Writing*, an anti-fascist magazine, on 27 May 1936, Orwell proposed writing a 2,000-3,000 word 'sketch' about 'the shooting of an elephant' for the journal, mentioning: 'It all came back to me very vividly the other day...' (1968 [1936]b: 250). Is it possible that it 'came back' to him 'vividly' because he had recently read Campbell's *Teak Wallah*, released the previous year, which included an anecdote about a man named Orwell who was faced with the prospect of having to shoot an elephant against his will? May this have inspired him to explore the alternative outcome to an encounter between someone like 'Orwell', Campbell's heroic teak wallah, and the musthing elephant he was charged with containing? Is it possible that Orwell, the more gifted writer, had immediately recognised how this slight twist in Campbell's familiar 'rogue elephant' theme, combined with his own carefully-crafted prose, would produce an infinitely more powerful reading experience, one that might even express a truth independent of factual reality? And if so, how, then, do we square that 'truth' if the essay is, in fact, just a story? These questions, of course, may never be definitively answered. Yet one thing seems certain: there is something distinctly Campbellian about the Burma works of Orwell. Is it not high time, then, that Reginald Campbell, alumnus of the Meggy School of Journalism, be recognised as an author who may have influenced the Burma writings of the young man who would later become the literary giant known the world over as George Orwell?

NOTES

[1] Childhood friend Jacintha Buddicom describes how, even as a child, Eric Blair predicted he would one day write 'not merely as an author, always a "FAMOUS AUTHOR", in capitals' (2006 [1974]: 38)

[2] 'Why I Joined the Independent Labour Party' (1982 [1938]a: 373-375) and a review of Frank Jellinek's *The Civil War in Spain* (1982 [1938]b: 376-380), for example, were published in the *New Leader*. In an 'As I Please' column, however, Orwell includes the *New Leader* in a list of publications in which 'bad English, Marxist English, or pamphletese' can be found (1968: 109)

[3] Orwell uses a variant spelling, eliminating the final 'h'

[4] One scholar, believing Campbell had 'a forest-manager whose *real* name was Orwell', noted that his 'method of dealing with an elephant in *musth* was a lot less catastrophic'. He thus wondered: 'Can it be that the cathartic report of George Orwell/Eric Blair was a fiction?' (MacKenzie 1992: 513)

[5] *Poo Lorn of the Elephants* was published as *Elephant King* (1930) in the United States

[6] Indeed, even the 'devilish' appearance of the Indian coolie trampled by the elephant and most 'other corpses' Orwell's narrator had seen (ibid: 268) as well as the notion of wearing a 'mask' ('He wears a mask, and his face grows to fit it' [op cit: 269]) seem strangely reminiscent of a passage in Campbell's 1932 *Fear in the Forest:* 'The faithful boy of the meek brown eyes was there no longer; instead, the face of a devil was glaring up at him. Death had torn away the actor's mask, revealing the soul of a fiend' (p. 297)

[7] The same story also appears as 'Timber-Working Elephants in the Siamese Jungle' (1934b)

[8] Just as Orwell's narrator is armed with only an insufficient weapon ('an old .44 Winchester and much too small to kill an elephant' [op cit: 266]), the teak wallahs in several of Campbell's works face similar issues; see, for example, *Brown Wife – Or White?* (op cit: 253), *Teak Wallah* (op cit: 77), *Tiger Valley* (op cit: 101), *Jungle Night* (op cit: 188), *This Animal Is Dangerous* (1934a: 127), and 'The Shikari' (1928b: 13)

[9] Maung Htin Aung (1970) claims that this incident was based on an actual event involving Orwell and a group of students at a train station in Rangoon. Htin Aung claims that while clowning around, one of the boys accidentally bumped into Blair, causing him to tumble down the stairs. As he tells it, 'Blair was furious and raised the heavy cane which he was carrying, to hit the boy on the head, but checked himself, and struck him on the back instead' (ibid: 23). The veracity of his claims, however, has been challenged; Jeffrey Meyers (2010), for example, says this apparently eyewitness account seems 'more like nationalist propaganda than an actual event' (ibid: 11)

[10] Bernard Crick (1982 [1980]) points out that one of the perks of Orwell's posting to Syriam was its proximity to Rangoon and to Smart and Mookerdum's Bookshop (ibid: 157)

[11] Reviews of Campbell's novels appeared in the *Folkestone Herald, Hastings and St Leonard's Observer,* the *Western Morning News and Daily Gazette,* the *Dundee Courier,* the *Middlesex County Times, Western Mail* and the *Cheltenham Chronicle and Gloucestershire Graphic,* among numerous others

[12] A series of articles entitled 'Teak Wallah', for example, was published in *Pearson's* before the publication of Campbell's memoir by the same title in 1935 ('Town Talk: Teak-Wallah' 1935: 2)

[13] Campbell's short stories, for example, have been anthologised in *Fifty Enthralling Stories of the Mysterious East* (n.d.) and *The Book of a Thousand Thrills* (1935)

[14] The origins of the street name, however, are no longer widely known among residents of Moulmein. Emma Larkin notes that when asked about its meaning, a Moulmein local confidently explains that the name means 'Orange-Shelf Street' (2005: 183)

[15] In Campbell's *Elephant King*, (published as *Poo Lorn of the Elephants* in the UK), teak wallah Cairns decides not to shoot the rampaging Poo Lorn and is thus forced 'to bear the stigma of being thought a coward' (op cit: 166). When someone later insinuates that he is afraid, another teak wallah jumps to his defence, saying: 'I've met him once or twice in the jungle and know him to be a man almost entirely without fear. I think he has shown this just now in a somewhat convincing manner.' The narrator elaborates: 'A hum of approval went round the assembly. It takes a brave man to face a charge of cowardice unflinchingly' (1930: 171)

REFERENCES

1901 England Census, *Ancestry.com* [database on-line], Provo, UT, USA: Ancestry.com Operations Inc., 2005

1911 England Census, *Ancestry.com* [database on-line], Provo, UT, USA: Ancestry.com Operations, Inc., 2011

Abbott, Gerry (2016) The poet who wanted to shoot an elephant, *George Orwell Studies,* Vol. 1, No. 1 pp 116-123

Allen, Sandy (2013) 17 personal essays that will change your life, *BuzzFeed,* 26 August. Available online at https://www.buzzfeed.com/sandraeallen/17-personal-essays-that-will-change-your-life, accessed on 7 December 2019

Aung, Maung Htin (1970) George Orwell and Burma, *Asian Affairs*, Vol. 1, No. 1, pp 19-28

Bexhill-on-Sea Observer (1935) 'Town Talk: Teak-Wallah', 13 July p. 2

Biederstadt, Carol (2019) George Orwell's *Burmese Days*: The case for a hybridised 'Florwell', *Orwell Society Journal*, No. 15 pp 10-13

Buddicom, Jacintha (2006 [1974]) *Eric & Us,* Chichester: Finlay Publisher

Campbell, Reginald (1925) *Brown Wife – Or White?* London: Chapman & Hall

Campbell, Reginald (1927) Just to add interest, *Everybody's,* Vol. LVI, No. 4, April pp 159-164

Campbell, Reginald (1928) The mankiller of Ai Poy and the humbling of the mighty, *Everybody's,* Vol. LIX, No. 1, July pp 83-89

Campbell, Reginald (1926a) My literary career, *New Leader,* Vol. XIII, No 27, 2 April p. 5

Campbell, Reginald (1926b) *Uneasy Virtue: A Tale of Northern Siam,* London: Chapman & Hall

Campbell, Reginald (1928a) Prestige, *Everybody's,* Vol. LVIII, No. 1, Jan pp 123-129

Campbell, Reginald (1928b) The shikari, *Everybody's,* Vol. LVIII, No. 4, April pp 11-15

Campbell, Reginald (1930a) *Poo Lorn of the Elephants,* London: Hodder & Stoughton

Campbell, Reginald (1930b) The humbling of Ai Poy and Ai Soo, *Sketch,* Vol. 152, No. 1971, 5 November pp 264, XVIII, XX

Campbell, Reginald (1931) *Tiger Valley,* New York: Richard R. Smith, Inc.

Campbell, Reginald (1932) *Fear in the Forest,* London: Hodder & Stoughton

Campbell, Reginald (1933) *Jungle Night,* London: Hodder & Stoughton

Campbell, Reginald (1934a) *This Animal Is Dangerous,* London: Hodder & Stoughton

Campbell, Reginald (1934b) Timber-working elephants in the Siamese jungle, *Cheltenham Chronicle and Gloucestershire Graphic,* 21 July p. 3

Campbell, Reginald (1937 [1935]) *Teak-Wallah,* London: Hodder & Stoughton

Crick, Bernard (1982 [1980]) *George Orwell: A Life,* Harmondsworth, Middlesex: Penguin

Davison, Peter (1998) *The Complete Works of George Orwell, Vol. 10: A Kind of Compulsion,* London: Secker & Warburg

Davison, Peter (1996) *George Orwell: A Literary Life,* New York: St. Martin's

Directors' Minute Book 1923-1927, London Metropolitan Archives, City of London, CLC/B/123/MS27008/006, from the Inchcape Group, Anglo-Thai Corporation

The Directory for Bangkok and Siam (1921) Bangkok: Bangkok Times Press

The Directory for Bangkok and Siam (1924) Bangkok: Bangkok Times Press

Fifty Enthralling Stories of the Mysterious East (n.d.) Bombay: The Times of India

Goonetilleke, D. C. R. A. (1982) George Orwell's *Burmese Days*: The novelist as reformer, *Kalyanī: Journal of Humanities & Social Sciences of the University of Kelaniya,* Vol. 1, Nos. 1-2 pp 182-194

Ingle, Stephen (1993) *George Orwell: A Political Life,* Manchester: Manchester University Press

Langham-Carter, R. R. (1947) *Old Moulmein, 875-1880,* Moulmein: The Moulmein Sun Press

CAROL BIEDERSTADT

Larkin, Emma (2005) *Finding George Orwell in Burma,* New York: Penguin

London, England, Church of England Births and Baptisms, 1813-1917 *Ancestry. com* [database on-line]. Provo, UT, USA: Ancestry.com Operations, Inc., 2010

London, England, Church of England Marriages and Banns, 1754-1932, *Ancestry.com* [database on-line]. Provo, UT, USA: Ancestry.com Operations, Inc., 2010

MacKenzie, John M. (1992) Review: The view from beyond, *International History Review,* Vol. 14, No. 3, August pp 503-517

Meyers, Jeffrey (2010) *Orwell: Life and Art,* Urbana: University of Illinois

National Archives, Kew, Admiralty, Navy, Royal Marines and Coastguard, ADM 196/174/31

Nisbet, Hugh (1935) *Experiences of a Jungle-Wallah,* St. Alban's: Fisher, Knight, & Co.

OCLC WorldCat Identities (2019) Campbell, Reginald 1894-1950, *worldcat. org*. Available online at: http://www.worldcat.org/identities/lccn-n85-361457/, accessed on 10 November 2019

Orwell, George (1989 [1934]) *Burmese Days,* London: Penguin

Orwell, George (1982 [1936]a) Shooting an Elephant, *The Collected Essays, Journalism and Letters of George Orwell, Vol. 1: An Age Like This 1920-1940,* London: Penguin pp 265-272; first published *New Writing*, No. 2, autumn

Orwell, George (1982 [1936]b) Letter to John Lehmann, *Collected Essays, Journalism and Letters of George Orwell Vol. 1: An Age Like This 1920-1940,* London: Penguin p. 250;

Orwell, George (1982 [1938]a) Why I joined the Independent Labour Party, *Collected Essays, Journalism and Letters of George Orwell, Vol. 1: An Age Like This 1920-1940,* London: Penguin pp 373-375; first published *New Leader*, 24 June

Orwell George (1982 [1938]b) Review: *The Civil War in Spain, Collected Essays, Journalism and Letters of George Orwell, Vol. 1: An Age Like This 1920-1940,* London: Penguin pp 376-380; first published, *New Leader,* 8 July

Orwell, George (1968 [1944]) As I Please, *Collected Essays, Journalism and Letters of George Orwell Vol. 3: As I Please 1943-1945,* New York: Harcourt Brace Jovanovich pp 108-111; first published 4 February

Rees, Richard (1962) *George Orwell: Fugitive from the Camp of Victory,* Carbondale: Southern Illinois University

Reyzer, Rafal (2016) 40 best essays of all time, *rafalreyzer.com,* 5 May. Available online at https://rafalreyzer.com/40-best-essays-of-all-time/, accessed on 7 December 2019

Rodden, John (2014) 'A Hanging': George Orwell's unheralded literary breakthrough, *Concentric: Literary and Cultural Studies,* Vol. 40, No. 1, March pp 19-33

Rose, Jonathan (1992) The invisible sources of *Nineteen Eighty-Four,* Rose, Jonathan (ed.) *The Revised Orwell,* East Lansing: Michigan State University pp 131-147

Saha, Jonathan (2017) Colonizing elephants: Animal agency, undead capital and imperial science in British Burma, *BJHS Themes 2*, 1 January. Available online at http://creativecommons.org/licenses/by/4.0/, accessed on 22 June 2019

Stansky, Peter and Abrahams, William (1972) *The Unknown Orwell,* New York: Alfred A. Knopf

Temple, Emily (2017) The most anthologized essays of the last 25 years, *Literary Hub,* 31 July. Available online at https://lithub.com/the-most-anthologized-essays-of-the-last-25-years/, accessed on 5 December 2019

Travers-Murison, James (2019) *Fred in Siam's Jungle: A Young Teak Wallah's Journal 1922-25, enligtenart.com* (Kindle book), Nymboida, Australia

UK, Incoming Passenger Lists, 1878-1960, *Ancestry.com* [database on-line]. Provo, UT, USA: Ancestry.com Operations Inc., 2008

Wattananikorn, Kittichai (2018) *British Teak Wallahs in Northern Thailand from 1876-1956,* Bangkok: White Lotus

Wattananikorn, Kittichai (2019) Personal communication

NOTE ON THE CONTRIBUTOR

Carol Biederstadt is an Associate Professor of English at Union County College in Cranford, NJ, USA.

PAPER

Orwell's Evil-Scepticism

PETER BRIAN BARRY

While George Orwell speaks of evil regularly, there is a strong case to be made that he is an evil-sceptic – doubting whether there is very much evil in the actual world. Orwell implicitly offers three arguments for some version of evil-scepticism: one flows from his understanding of meaningless language expressed in 'Politics and Language'; the second emerges from the conception of the evil person that he seems to favour, albeit a conception that he appears to think is never realised in reality; the third is based upon Orwell's fears about how normative language may be abused. Perhaps surprisingly, a fair reading of Orwell's corpus suggests that he is deeply sceptical about the existence of evil and evil people.

Keywords: George Orwell, evil, evil-scepticism, extreme, power

> But born, alas, in an evil time,
> I missed that pleasant haven,
> For the hair has grown on my upper lip
> And the clergy are all clean-shaven (*CWGO* 1: 524).[1]

George Orwell often laments that he lives in an age ill-aligned with goodness. 'So far as we can see,' he tells us, 'both horror and pain are necessary to the continuance of life on this planet' (*CWGO* 18: 430) and 'on balance life is suffering' (*CWGO* 19: 64). But in his poem 'A Happy Vicar I Might Have Been', he does not bemoan that he lives in a bad or sorrowful time, but an *evil* time. No surprise Orwell 'firmly believed' that an 'evil destiny' awaits him (*CWGO* 19: 382). What other destiny befits one born into an evil time?

Rush Rees notes the frequency with which Orwell uses 'evil' (1962: 33) which belies the conclusion that Orwell is best understood as an advocate of *evil scepticism*. While their favoured view admits of some variations, evil sceptics are united in thinking that 'there is much less evil in the real world than is commonly thought' (Russell 2006: 90). It might be thought that Orwell's evil-scepticism has a basis in his ambivalence towards religion generally and Roman Catholicism in particular (Brennan 2017). On some accounts, philosophers have avoided talking about it since 'evil is so intimately tied to religious discourse' (Bernstein 2005: 4) but it is far from clear that the concept of evil must be tied to religion or religious doctrine (Barry 2013). And in any case, Orwell implicitly offers three arguments for evil-scepticism that have little to do with any supposed connection between evil and religious thought, arguments that contemporary evil-sceptics have not acknowledged. The discussion below is largely expository, occasionally critical, and makes the case that Orwell is most plausibly read as decidedly ambivalent about the existence of evil and evil people.

TWO SENSES OF 'EVIL'

The primary obstacle to classifying Orwell as an evil-sceptic is that, as Rees notes, he uses 'evil' so often and in some of his most important fiction, essays, reviews and journalism. Early in his service in the British Raj, Orwell explains: 'I had already made up my mind that imperialism was an evil thing and the sooner I chucked up my job and got out of it the better' (*CWGO* 10: 501). The exploitation of a hundred million Indians for English comfort is 'an evil state of affairs' (*CWGO* 5: 148) and Crown rule in India is 'evil despotism' (ibid: 138). He holds that 'capitalism is evil' (ibid: 202) – indeed, 'inherently evil' (*CWGO* 12: 460) – and that socialism requires thinking that 'most of the evil that men do results from the warping effects of injustice and inequality' (*CWGO* 18: 63). Poverty is evil not because 'it makes a man suffer' but because 'it rots him physically and spiritually' (*CWGO* 1: 206-207). Killing is not necessarily evil; what is 'truly evil' is to 'act in such a way that peaceful life becomes impossible' (*CWGO* 12: 317). These are not just idle musings; they are expressions of Orwell's deepest moral and political commitments.

Still, Orwell uses 'evil' equivocally. In his novel *Burmese Days* (1934), the snobbish Elizabeth regards the choice to live as a penniless artist as 'shameful, degrading, evil' (*CWGO* 2: 96) and she is put off by the condition of her mother's unkept studio which 'was more than depressing … it was evil' (ibid: 94). Elizabeth betrays her bourgeois sentiments and perhaps Orwell's own. As many commentators note, Orwell was easily disgusted, especially by noxious odours and stenches (Bowker 2003: 198; Crick 1980: 19; Rees 1962: 33; Stansky and Abrahams 1972: 22). Readers are treated to descriptions of evil-smelling kitchens (*CWGO* 3: 51), glue pots (*CWGO* 3: 295), flights of stairs (*CWGO* 4: 28 and 247), sinks (*CWGO* 4: 231), barns (*CWGO* 6: 200), and holding cells (*CWGO* 9: 238). He cannot reminisce about his schooldays without 'seeming to breathe in a whiff of something cold and evil-smelling' (*CWGO* 19: 370). In his novel, *Keep the Aspidistra Flying* (1936), Gordon Comstock's boss is an 'evil-looking creature' (*CWGO* 4: 222) as is a cross-eyed chambermaid (ibid: 195); even red and blue neon lights look evil (ibid: 175) and 'evil brown grass' grows over slag heaps in

PETER BRIAN BARRY

the North (*CWGO* 5: 97); Spanish trench-mortars make 'the most evil sound of all' (*CWGO* 6: 61); while the food in *Nineteen Eighty-Four*'s Oceania tastes evil (*CWGO* 9: 63).

It is difficult to believe that Orwell means the same thing when he suggests that both exploitation and rank sinks are evil. This is not necessarily indicative of a misunderstanding on his part: 'evil', the word, is ambiguous and admits of more than one sense. The primary definition offered by the *Oxford English Dictionary* states that 'evil' is 'the antithesis of good in all its principal senses,' the most comprehensive adjectival expression of disapproval in English. This is the *ordinary sense* according to which 'evil' is synonymous with 'bad', nothing more (Barry 2013: 13). By contrast, in the *extreme sense*, 'evil' is a superlative, the strongest term for expressing moral condemnation in the English language (ibid: 13) and 'the worst possible term of opprobrium imaginable' (Singer, Marcus 2004: 185). So understood, evil people are not just bad people but the morally worst sort of person (Barry 2013: 13), evil actions are not just wrongful but 'the worst wrongs people do' (Card 2002: 28), and so on.

Orwell's frequent use of 'evil' is no obstacle to evil-scepticism if he usually means to invoke its ordinary sense. And clearly, he often does. For example, he identifies various 'minor evils' that plague tramps, including the 'discomfort, which is inseparable from life on the road' (*CWGO* 1: 207), evils that are lesser in comparison to the 'especial' evils that plague tramps including hunger, celibacy and enforced idleness (ibid: 205). Physical discomfort while tramping is bad but not evil in the extreme sense if other deprivations are much, much worse. Consider, too, what Orwell has to say in his 1948 essay 'Writers and Leviathan':

> … most of us still have a lingering belief that every choice, even political choice, is between good and evil, and that if a thing is necessary it is also right. We should, I think, get rid of this belief, which belongs in the nursery. In politics one can never do more than decide which of two evils is the lesser, and there are some situations from which one can only escape by acting like a devil or a lunatic (*CWGO* 19: 292).

Talk of choosing between evils is commonplace in Orwell's writing: he justifies war with Germany in his 1941 *Adelphi* essay, 'No, Not One', on the grounds that 'You can let the Nazis rule the world, that is evil; or you can overthrow them by war, which is also evil' (*CWGO* 13: 43) and he speculates generally that 'perhaps the choice before man is always a choice of evils' (*CWGO* 16: 400). Nothing wrong with talk of lesser evils – in 1924, the young Eric Blair titled one of his better poems 'The Lesser Evil' (*CWGO* 10: 92-93) – but such talk only makes sense if the ordinary sense is used: lesser evils are, well, lesser in comparison to greater evils such that 'evil' could not function as a superlative. In the extreme sense, talk of lesser evils is a misnomer.[2] So, if politics invariably requires us to consider lesser evils, then, given that politics permeates his writing, the default assumption should probably be that Orwell intends the ordinary sense when he uses 'evil'.

None of this shows that Orwell is an evil sceptic, but it suggests that his frequent use of 'evil' does not show that he thinks there is very much evil in the world, properly understood. But Orwell does implicitly offer at least three arguments that suggest that he *is* an evil sceptic. I consider each of these arguments in the next three sections below.

'EVIL' AS A MEANINGLESS WORD

Contemporary evil sceptics suggest variously that 'it is ultimately not possible to understand evil' (Morrow 2003: 3), that 'The essence of evil … is elusive and indefinable' (ibid: 21), that 'evil in the end is always the inexplicable' (Ellwood 2009: 4), that 'The notion that we could with consistency locate the line that separates the justifiably bad from the inexcusably evil … is ridiculous' (Flescher 2013: 5), that evil is properly equated with something 'unspeakable' (Eagleton 2010: 17) and that we are 'at a loss to define what we mean' (Bernstein 2005:1) when we talk about evil. All of this at least suggests that 'evil' is, in some sense, a meaningless word. Orwell never explicitly classifies 'evil' as meaningless, aside from his complaint about the 'woolly vagueness of a passage' (*CWGO* 12: 30) of Dickens in which 'evil' appears. But his stated position is that meaningless words should be consigned to the dustbin (*CWGO* 17: 430). If 'evil' is meaningless for reasons that Orwell himself offers, then he is committed to commending its purgation from our vernacular, a kind of victory for the evil sceptic.

In his 1946 essay, 'Politics and the English Language', Orwell includes meaningless words in his 'catalogue of swindles and perversions' (*CWGO* 17: 425). He offers some examples of meaningless words below, but also suggests just what suffices for meaninglessness:

> The word *Fascism* has now no meaning except in so far as it signifies 'something not desirable'. The words *democracy, socialism, freedom, patriotic, realistic, justice,* have each of them several different meanings which cannot be reconciled with one another. In the case of a word like *democracy*, not only is there no agreed definition, but the attempt to make one is resisted from all sides. It is almost universally felt that when we call a country democratic we are praising it: consequently the defenders of every kind of regime claim that it is a democracy, and fear that they might have to stop using the word if it were tied down to any one meaning. Words of this kind are often

used in a consciously dishonest way. That is, the person who uses them has his own private definition but allows his hearer to think he means something quite different (ibid).

Orwell, here, identifies at least four criteria of meaninglessness: first, meaningless words signify nothing but that their object is 'something not desirable'; second, there is no agreement about their definition; third, attempts to secure agreement are resisted 'from all sides'; fourth, they are 'often used in a consciously dishonest way'. It is unclear if these criteria are individually or jointly sufficient conditions for meaninglessness, a philosopher's cavil. But certainly if 'evil' meets all these criteria, then Orwell is committed to regarding it as meaningless.

Consider Orwell's first criterion: meaningless words signify nothing but that their object is not desirable. Orwell worries elsewhere that normative language is in danger of losing its meaning if it only signifies approval or disapproval: 'if one says ... that *King Lear* is a good play and *The Four Just Men* is a good thriller' then 'what meaning is there in the word "good"?' (CWGO 18: 302). It is more precise to say that Orwell worries that normative language risks becoming meaningless when it has only *emotive* meaning. As Orwell wrote, emotivism had emerged as an influential philosophical theory about the nature of morality and moral language. Emotivism's signature thesis is that when we engage in moral discourse we are not primarily asserting moral propositions expressive of beliefs; rather, we are primarily expressing feelings and desires constitutive of approval or disapproval. For various reasons, Orwell is not well regarded as an emotivist. A. J. Ayer, himself an emotivist (Ayer 1936), noted Orwell's lack of interest in abstract philosophy such as metaethics (Ayer 1977). Emotivists also typically deny the existence of those universal moral norms that Orwell had 'strong confidence in' (Dwan 2018: 15). But emotivists draw a distinction that is illuminating: a leading advocate of emotivism, Charles Stevenson, distinguishes different kinds of meaning by distinguishing the 'psychological reactions' of those who use language (Stevenson 1944: 42). The emotive meaning of a term is, roughly, a function of non-cognitive attitudes like desires and feelings, those attitudes whose nature is that of being for or against something (Stevenson 1937). Determining just what the emotive meaning of a term is will be a task for cultural anthropologists: it requires discovering which desires and feelings a linguistic community will tend to have when the term in question is used. By contrast, the descriptive meaning of a term is, roughly, a function of the cognitive attitudes that an audience is disposed to have given use of the term in question. To discern the descriptive meaning of some term, a cultural anthropologist will have to determine what beliefs, for example, a linguistic community will tend to have when the term in question is used.

If Orwell is right that 'fascism' signifies only that 'something is not desirable', it may lack descriptive meaning but it retains its emotive meaning since its use tends to produce the requisite attitude of disapproval. Similarly, 'democracy' has emotive meaning if it is used solely as a vehicle to offer praise, even if it lacks descriptive meaning. Orwell, then, appears to endorse the following theory of meaning: emotive meaning is not enough for meaningfulness; language lacking descriptive meaning is meaningless simpliciter.

Ascribing to Orwell this theory of meaning helps to clarify what he says about meaninglessness in 'Politics and the English Language'. Consider first Orwell's suggestion that meaningless words lack an agreed-upon definition. If there is no agreed-upon definition of some term, then we have good reason to doubt that there are any cognitive attitudes that a linguistic community will be disposed to have when that term is used. So, the absence of an agreed-upon definition about a term suggests that it lacks descriptive meaning. Similarly, if attempts to secure agreement about the definition of a term are resisted from all sides, then a linguistic community will not tend to have any particular cognitive attitudes in response to the use of a term. Resistance to definitions will also undermine descriptive meaning. It appears, then, that while Orwell initially offers four different criteria of meaningless, he essentially endorses a general theory of meaning.

With this theory of meaning in place, it is possible to argue that Orwell is committed to supposing that 'evil' is meaningless – at least 'evil' is meaningless on Orwellian grounds if 'fascism' and 'democracy' are. Generally, there is a strong case to be made that 'evil' meets all four criteria of meaninglessness that Orwell identifies and therefore lacks descriptive meaning. First, 'evil' has arguably come to function only as a vehicle to signify one's disapproval – if, say, it has come 'to represent everything that one hates and despises, what one takes to be vile and despicable' (Bernstein 2002: 3). Second, as noted above, there is clearly disagreement about what 'evil' means, suggesting that there is no agreed definition. Third, various regimes have resisted clarifying what 'evil' means, presumably to continue to use it as they see fit.[3] Finally, there can be little doubt that 'evil' is sometimes used in a consciously dishonest way – say, 'as a political tool to obscure complex issues, to block genuine thinking, and to stifle public discussion and debate' (Bernstein 2005: vii). So, there is at least a strong case to be made that 'evil' meets all four of Orwell's criteria for meaninglessness. And if Orwell does think that meaningless words should be purged from our vernacular, then 'evil' should be purged *ipso facto*, a kind of victory for the evil sceptic.

A *tu quoque* response is clearly available: after all, Orwell did not actually suspend his use of 'fascism' and 'democracy' and other

PAPER

PETER BRIAN BARRY

purportedly meaningless language. Better responses will abandon Orwell's theory of meaning or his contention that 'evil' lacks descriptive meaning. But whether or not Orwell's first argument for evil-scepticism is sound, he does implicitly argue for evil-scepticism. He has at least two other, different arguments for evil-scepticism as well.

THE ORWELLIAN CONCEPTION OF EVIL PERSONHOOD

Most of us are sceptics about unicorns. It is not that we don't understand what a unicorn *is*; rather, we understand, more or less, what unicorns are and we doubt that there is anything like that. Perhaps there are fictional unicorns in the worlds of fantasy. But, if there is nothing in the actual world like that, then there are no actual unicorns. Thus, unicorn-scepticism is born.

Some evil-sceptics offer a similarly structured argument. Philip Cole entertains the thought that for someone to be genuinely evil, they must be literally monstrous. On this *monstrous* conception of evil personhood, evil people literally lack the nature possessed by human beings (Cole 2006: 13). Perhaps there are fictional monstrous people in distant possible worlds. But, if no one in the actual world is monstrous, then there are no actual evil people. Thus, evil-scepticism. I submit that Orwell anticipates this argument: he articulates a conception of evil personhood – an account of what evil people are like – albeit a conception that he seems to doubt is ever realised in the actual world. The result is scepticism about the existence of evil people.

What, according to Orwell, makes someone evil? Orwell nowhere answers this question explicitly but some of his fictional characters are linked to the notion of evil. One such character is U Po Kyin, the 'evil Burmese magistrate' (Stansky and Abrahams 1979: 59) of *Burmese Days*. He is called a scoundrel and a crocodile (*CWGO* 2: 44) and he is described as having 'done very much evil' (ibid: 12), as 'planning some evil' (ibid), and as the architect of 'a base, evil plan' (ibid: 144). His wife, Ma Kin, wonders 'why is it that you are only happy when you are being wicked? Why is it that everything you do must bring evil to others?' (ibid: 144). By the novel's end, he has gained membership to the xenophobic Kyauktada Club, 'the very highest honour an Oriental can attain to' (ibid: 146). He is promoted, decorated and honoured by Indians and the British alike having 'done all that mortal man could do', dying before building a host of pagodas in the hope of avoiding comeuppance for his evildoing (ibid: 298). Early in the novel, Ma Kin questions his motives, asking: 'Ko Po Kyin, you have grown rich and powerful and what good has it ever done you?' (ibid: 12). He denies having any interest in money, ultimately revealing that he longs to feel like he has 'risen in the world' (ibid: 146). His backstory suggests that what he really wants is power: a young U Po Kyin had witnessed the march of seemingly omnipotent British troops through Mandalay and acquired as 'his ruling ambition' a desire to fight with the British (ibid: 2). Orwell's description of U Po Kyin is also suggestive: he revels in his corpulence, knowing that he 'was now fat, rich and feared' and imagines that he is 'swollen with the bodies of his enemies' (ibid: 11).

U Po Kyin is hardly the only character from Orwell's corpus who is rightly regarded as evil. Arguably, if any of Orwell's characters are evil it is O'Brien, the philosopher-enforcer of the Party in *Nineteen Eighty-Four* who is twice called 'evil' by one of Orwell's biographers (Meyers 2000: 280 and 285). U Po Kyin's thirst for power and his lack of concern for those sacrificed along the way are also evident in O'Brien. After Winston proposes that the Party is committed to 'doing evil that good may come', O'Brien chides Winston for his 'stupid' proposal and offers an alternative explanation:

> The Party seeks power entirely for its own sake. We are not interested in the good of others; we are interested solely in power. Not wealth or luxury or long life or happiness: only power, pure power. What pure power means you will understand presently (*CWGO* 9: 275).

O'Brien is clear that 'Power is not a means, it is an end' (ibid: 276) and that what the Party wants intrinsically is power over human beings, 'above all, over the mind' (ibid: 277). Some of Orwell's readers are sceptical here. Rees thought 'the power philosophy of the Party is presented in fantastic and almost hysterical terms' (1962: 104). Crick twice suggests that Orwell might simply be satirising the power-hungry (1980: 322 and 399). Alex Zwerdling regards Orwell's ruminations about power as an 'irrational element in Orwell's belief' (1974: 104). In defence of this scepticism, note that Orwell suggests that he meant to parody totalitarianism's intellectual implications (*CWGO* 19: 487). Yet Orwell often expressed concern about the desire for power for its own sake. For instance, he worried that 'The desire for pure power seems to be much more dominant than the desire for wealth' (*CWGO* 18:504) and that his contemporaries were aligning themselves with a 'cult of power,' one 'mixed up with a love cruelty and wickedness for their own sakes' (*CWGO* 16: 354). In his 1939 *Adelphi* review of Bertrand Russell's *Power*, Orwell concedes that 'at present the rule of naked force obtains almost everywhere' and that probably 'has always been the case' (*CWGO* 11: 311). On this basis, other commentators are inclined to take Orwell at his word. David Wykes attributes to Orwell 'a reluctant awareness that the power drive might actually be a psychic compulsion' (1987: 78).

If the desire for power for its own sake is neither new nor uncommon, it might still distinguish evil people from the rest of us. In the penultimate paragraph of his review of *Nineteen Eighty-Four*,

PETER BRIAN BARRY

Philip Rahv offers the cryptic remark that 'Evil, far more than good, is in need of the pseudo-religious justifications so readily provided by the ideologies of world-salvation and compulsory happiness' (1975: 272). As such, 'the Grand Inquisitors of the world are compelled … to believe in the fiction that their power is merely a means to some other end gratifying and noble' (ibid: 273). Well, maybe. But perhaps, in moments, genuinely evil characters drop the pretence and acknowledge just why they do what they do. What is shocking about U Po Kyin and O'Brien is not just their willingness to say what they want, but their insouciance with moralising that purports to challenge them: they share a radical thirst for power itself and a deep callousness about the consequences of its pursuit. They are not merely vicious but *virulently vicious* (Barry 2016). And together, they suggest a template for understanding the evil person: evil people greatly want power for its own sake and lack any compunction about pursuing it. Call this the *Orwellian conception of evil personhood*.

Orwell's own fictional creations may then be 'evil'. Yet he seems disinclined to call his fellow, actual human beings 'evil' as, say, U Po Kyin or O'Brien. Orwell describes Hitler as a 'monomaniac' and assures us that 'I would certainly kill him if I could get within reach of him' but he admits that 'I have never been able to dislike Hitler,' that 'I could feel no personal animosity' towards him, even that 'there is something deeply appealing' about him (*CWGO* 12:117). Neither the Spanish fascists nor the communists who betrayed the men fighting alongside Orwell in the POUM militia are called 'evil' in *Homage to Catalonia* (1938): Orwell has 'the most evil memories of Spain, but … very few bad memories of Spaniards' (*CWGO* 6: 178). The opinions disseminated by Ezra Pound may be 'evil ones' (*CWGO* 20:102) but Orwell does not conclude that Pound himself is evil. Orwell does regard an English archetype as evil: 'The hanging judge, that evil old man in scarlet robe and horse-hair wig, whom nothing short of dynamite will ever teach what century he is living in' (*CWGO* 12: 307). But I am aware of nowhere that Orwell calls another person 'evil'.

There is, then, a curious ambivalence in Orwell: he endorses a conception of evil personhood yet consistently declines to apply it to actual people. This ambivalence suggests Orwell's second argument for evil-scepticism: to be an evil person like O'Brien is both to want power for its own sake and lack any compunction in its pursuit. But, apparently, there are no actual people like that. Thus, Orwell's scepticism about evil people.

The plausibility of Orwell's second sceptical argument turns partly on the plausibility of the Orwellian conception. Orwell complained about the crude moral psychology of Marxists who suppose that we always and only act in pursuit of economic interests: 'The main weakness of Marxism,' he explained, 'is its failure to interpret human motives' (*CWGO* 12: 244) thereby ignoring other possible motives, including religion and patriotism that are not clearly reducible to economic interests. But supposing that evil people act only for the sake of securing power is no less crude, ignoring the possibility that evil people might act for more familiar motives, including profit or pleasure – or just for the hell of it. The plausibility of the Orwellian conception also turns on the empirical reality of putative real-life evil people. Different readers will have to decide for themselves whether the naked and unapologetic desire for power is fictional or all-too real. In any case, Orwell offers a second argument for evil-scepticism, one that questions the very existence of evil people. He has still another argument available.

DRAGON HUNTING AND EVIL-SCEPTICISM

If there is any occasion in which Orwell clearly intends the extreme sense of 'evil,' it is at the end of *Nineteen Eighty-Four*. In its final pages, the broken Winston is left to get drunk and work though chess puzzles:

> He examined the chess problem and set out the pieces. It was a tricky ending, involving a couple of knights. 'White to play and mate in two moves.' Winston looked up at the portrait of Big Brother. White always mates, he thought with a sort of cloudy mysticism. Always, without exception, it is so arranged. In no chess problem since the beginning of the world has black ever won. Did it not symbolize the eternal, unvarying triumph of Good over Evil? The huge face gazed back at him, full of calm power. White always mates (*CWGO* 9: 302).

A bit later, a war bulletin announces a breakthrough in Oceania's war against Eurasia and Winston imagines a 'white arrow tearing across the tail of the black' (ibid: 310) – the forces of Oceania represented by white, those of Eurasia by black. Orwell, then, identifies white and black, not with good and evil, but Good and Evil, a seemingly deliberate use of capitalisation by Orwell.[4] But to what end?

Elsewhere, when Orwell capitalises in this way, he does so ironically. Consider his comments in his essay 'Culture and Democracy', of 1941:

> Six months ago, Stalin was Bad with a big B. Now he is Good with a big G. A year ago the Finns were Good. Now they are Bad. Mussolini is Bad at this moment but it would not particularly surprise me to see him Good within a year... (*CWGO* 13: 78).

It is easy to read Orwell here as complaining about a tendency of his contemporaries to engage in hyperbole. If one calls one's allies and enemies 'good' and 'bad', one has not praised and blamed them enough. Only 'Good' and 'Bad', with capital letters for emphasis, are adequate for the task. *Nineteen Eighty-Four* demonstrates that this tendency is not just excessive or unnecessary, but dangerous. Consider how Oceania's enemies are represented: the poster campaign intended to produce a frenzy of patriotism among the proles includes a photograph of a Eurasian soldier portrayed as a 'monstrous figure' with an 'expressionless Mongolian face' (*CWGO* 9: 156); during Hate Week, a Party orator bellows a lengthy list of 'atrocities, massacres, deportations, lootings, rapings, torture of prisoners, bombing of civilians, lying propaganda, unjust aggressions, broken treaties' (ibid: 188) suffered by Oceania, the very worst of crimes that only an evil enemy could perpetrate; during the Two Minute Hate, Goldstein is identified as the 'primal traitor, the earliest defiler of the Party's purity' (ibid:14) and the assembled react to his image with 'uncontrollable exclamations of rage' (ibid: 15). Replacing emotions like compassion and love with emotions conducive to animosity, aggression and antagonism is 'O'Brien's cherished goal' according to Martha Nussbaum (2005: 281). And the whole point of this political theatre is to stir up hatred, aggression and fear, psychological states that do not tend to encourage reasoned and rational discourse but rather violence, war, suspicion, hatred and contempt.

A number of commentators worry about how the very use of the term 'evil' can poison relationships. Richard Bernstein complains of a 'vulgar Manichaeism' according to which whatever one thinks of as evil is to be 'violently extirpated' (2002: 3). Cole worries that characterising one's enemy as evil demands nothing less than their 'complete condemnation', a tactic that ensures 'the impossibility of communication and negotiation' (2006: 236). In other words, there are serious costs to calling others 'evil' which might favour abandoning talk of evil altogether – and this might amount to another kind of victory for the evil-sceptic.

This third sceptical argument resembles one that Orwell pursues elsewhere. On two occasions, he recalls an aphorism that he ascribes to Nietzsche that cautions those who hunt dragons to avoid becoming dragons themselves (*CWGO* 11: 113 and 16: 387).[5] On both occasions, Orwell worries that the viciousness of those who demonise and take revenge upon defeated Nazis too clearly resembles that of their former adversaries. In general, we should refrain from relating to our enemies in ways that make us more hateful and hostile, less compassionate and just. But that suggests that we should demur from talk of evil to ensure that we do not become more like those we loathe.

The most serious obstacle to this third argument for evil-scepticism is that it commends doing something that we have good reason not to do. Arguably, we *need* a superlative in our moral vernacular for purposes of especially strong moral condemnation: calling Hitler or the Holocaust 'bad' or even 'very, very bad' might seem too weak. Prefix your adjectives with as many 'verys' as you like; sometimes, only 'evil' will do (Haybron 2002: 260). Someone like Orwell who eschews purple prose in favour of 'prose like a windowpane' should value language that accurately represents its object; tepid moral language may fail in that regard whereas 'evil' in the extreme sense does rather better. Worse, there is arguably something morally dubious about classifying genuinely evil people as something less-than-evil: perhaps failing to condemn them adequately amounts to failing to show due concern for their moral depravity or adequate concern for their victims. Perhaps common decency demands naming evil people as such when we find them. Orwell appears to think otherwise given that he suggests that talk of 'evil' does more to obscure than to clarify. At least many contemporary evil-sceptics agree.

CONCLUSION

For various reasons and in spite of his prodigious use of 'evil', Orwell can be considered an evil-sceptic. This reading of Orwell suggests he held a somewhat rosier view of humanity than is sometimes appreciated. Again, while Orwell's memories of Spain are 'mostly evil' he, nonetheless, makes clear that 'the whole experience has left me with not less but more belief in the decency of human beings' (*CWGO* 6: 186), a belief that is difficult to reconcile with a thoroughgoing conviction that one's fellows are not just bad, but evil. Whether Orwell's evil-scepticism is ultimately persuasive is an open question; I confess to having doubts that it is.

NOTES

[1] George Orwell, 'A happy vicar I might have been', in *The Complete Works of George Orwell, Vol. 10: A Kind of Compulsion 1903-1936*, edited by Peter Davison (London: Secker & Warburg 1998: 524). All parenthetical citations are to the 20-volume *The Complete Works* (*CWGO*) edited by Peter Davison (London: Secker & Warburg, 1998) and indicate volume and page number

[2] In a similar vein, after noting that we sometimes use expressions like 'lesser of two evils', Richard Bernstein suggests that 'more often we think of evil in absolute terms' which rules out gradations (Bernstein 2005: 1-2)

[3] Peter Singer documents the frequency with which the President of the United States, George W. Bush, used 'evil' without ever quite explaining what he means by it (Singer, Peter 2004)

[4] Davison's textual note to *Nineteen Eighty-Four* does not suggest that this singular instance of capitalisation was the product of editorial discretion or some scrivener's error and thus appears to be Orwell's deliberate intention

[5] Orwell probably has Aphorism 146 from *Beyond Good and Evil* in mind where Nietzsche says: 'Whoever fights monsters should see to it that in the process he does not become a monster' (Nietzsche 1989 [1886]: 89)

PETER BRIAN BARRY

REFERENCES

Ayer, A. J. (1936) *Language, Truth, and Logic*, London: Victor Gollancz Ltd

Ayer, A. J. (1977) *Part of My Life*, London: Collins Ltd

Barry, Peter Brian (2013) *Evil and Moral Psychology*, New York: Routledge

Barry, Peter Brian (2016) *The Fiction of Evil*, New York: Routledge

Bernstein, Richard (2002) *Radical Evil: A Philosophical Interrogation*, Cambridge: Polity

Bernstein, Richard (2005) *The Abuse of Evil: The Corruption of Politics and Religion Since 9/11*, Malden, MA: Polity Press

Bowker, Gordon (2003) *Inside George Orwell,* New York: Palgrave

Brennan, Michael (2017) *George Orwell and Religion*, New York, Bloomsbury

Card, Claudia (2002) *The Atrocity Paradigm: A Theory of Evil*, Oxford: Oxford University Press

Cole, Philip (2006) *The Myth of Evil*, Edinburgh: Edinburgh University Press

Crick, Bernard (1980) *George Orwell: A Life*, Boston: Little, Brown and Company

Dwan, David (2018) *Liberty, Equality, and Humbug: Orwell's Political Ideals*, Oxford: Oxford University Press

Eagleton, Terry (2010) *On Evil*, New Haven, CT: Yale University Press

Ellwood, Robert (2009) *Tales of Darkness: The Mythology of Evil,* New York: Continuums

Flescher, Andrew Michael (2013) *Moral Evil*, Washington DC: Georgetown University Press

Haybron, Daniel (2002) Moral monsters and saints, *The Monist,* Vol. 85, No. 2 pp 260-284

Meyers, Jeffrey (2000) *Orwell: Wintry Conscience of a Generation,* New York: W. W. Norton & Co.

Morrow, James (2003) *Evil: An Investigation*, New York: Basic Books

Nietzsche, Friedrich (1989 [1886]) *Beyond Good and Evil: Prelude to a Philosophy of the Future* (trans. by Kaufmann, Walter), New York: Vintage

Nussbaum, Martha C. (2005) The death of pity: Orwell and American political life, Gleason, Abbott, Goldsmith, Jack and Nussbaum, Martha C. (eds) *On Nineteen Eighty-Four: Orwell and Our Future*, Princeton: Princeton University Press

Rahv, Philip (1975) The unfuture of Utopia, Jeffrey Myers (ed.) *George Orwell: The Critical Heritage*, London: Routledge and Kegan Paul

Rees, Rush (1962) *George Orwell: Fugitive from the Camp of Victory.* Carbondale, IL: Southern Illinois University Press

Russell, Luke (2006) Evil-revivalism versus evil-scepticism, *The Journal of Value Inquiry,* Vol. 40 pp 89-105

Singer, Marcus (2004) The concept of evil, *Philosophy* Vol. 79, No. 2 pp 185-214

Singer, Peter (2004) *The President of Good and Evil: The Ethics of George W. Bush*. New York: Penguin

Stansky, Peter and Abrahams, William (1972) *The Unknown Orwell*, New York: Knopf

Stansky, Peter and Abrahams, William (1979) *Orwell: The Transformation*, New York: Knopf

Stevenson, Charles (1937) The emotive meaning of ethical terms, *Mind*, Vol. 46, No. 181 pp 14-31

Stevenson, Charles (1944) *Ethics and Language*, New Haven: Yale University Press

Wykes, David (1987) *A Preface to Orwell*, London, Longman

Zwerdling, Alex (1974) *Orwell and the Left*, New Haven: Yale University Press

NOTE ON THE CONTRIBUTOR

Peter Brian Barry is Professor of Philosophy and the Finkbeiner Endowed Professor in Ethics at Saginaw Valley State University. He is the author of *Evil and Moral Psychology* (2013, Routledge) and *The Fiction of Evil* (2016, Routledge) and has authored chapters for the forthcoming *The Cambridge Companion to George Orwell's Nineteen Eighty-Four* and *The Oxford Handbook to George Orwell*. He writes and teaches at the intersection of philosophy and literature and is preparing a monograph on the ethical philosophy of George Orwell.

Orwell and Dress:
The Naked Truth?

RICHARD LANCE KEEBLE

Dress is important to Orwell. Clothes feature prominently in his writings – and while at times he enjoys adopting a shabby look he can also look quite a dandy. Significantly, it is this aspect of his personality that British intelligence found somewhat baffling when they were following him as he worked for the BBC in 1942 and which sculptor Martin Jennings highlights in his statue of Orwell unveiled at the BBC in 2017 (Kennedy 2017). This paper will take a look at Orwell's appearance (as revealed in photographs) and examine some of his many representations of dress in his journalism, essays, novels and poetry. It will also explore his depictions of people undressed and his awareness of both the symbolic and sexual power of the naked truth.

Keywords: George Orwell, dress, nakedness, 'The Spike', ***Down and Out in Paris and London, Homage to Catalonia,*** **'As I Please', John Berger**

> We are, everywhere, surrounded by ideas. For the most part, we unthinkingly suppose that they are to be found in the form of books and poems, visualised in buildings and paintings, exposited in philosophical propositions and mathematical deductions. … But what if clothes could be understood as ideas too, as fully formed and eloquent as any poem, painting or equation?
> **(Bari 2019: 12)**

ORWELL: THE TIE AND BEING METICULOUS ABOUT THE MOUSTACHE

The tie is the one feature of his dress that Orwell seems attached to throughout his life. The cravat, the thicker, neck scarf or bow tie (as, say, cultivated by the Russian spy, Donald Maclean, and Winston Churchill) never appealed and only rarely (such as on the frontline during the Spanish civil war in 1937) does he go open-necked. Working class, middle class, upper class and down-and-outs all wore the tie during Orwell's time. It was distinctly ordinary – so there was no particularly bourgeois element to his liking it. Rather, it reflects, perhaps, a liking for routine, consistency and maybe even tradition in Orwell who, though a radical and one-time revolutionary, held (like all of us) contradictory attitudes in many areas.

In all but four of the 17 photographs of Orwell in Gordon Bowker's biography (2003) he wears a tie: thus, with his father, mother and Avril in 1918; standing, proudly with an erect back, his hands gripping the top of a mallet, with friends Prosper and Guinever Buddicom when 14; on an Eton field day (with Cyril Connolly amongst others) in 1920; at the Mandalay Police Training School in 1923; even, surprisingly in his tramp's uniform and on the beach with the family dog, Hector; with his lover Mabel Fierz; when feeding the goat Muriel in the garden at his Wallington home; on the ILP summer school in 1937, working at the BBC and (looking rather relaxed and jovial), holding his son, Richard, in a London street. Significantly, one of the rare times he sports an open neck is when he is shown as a young lad smoking on his way back from swimming at 'Athens' on the Thames near Eton: and Bowker dubs him 'Orwell the delinquent' (ibid). This is also one of the very few times in which Orwell is shown wearing a hat.

His father, Richard Walmseley, on the other hand, it seems, loved wearing hats: Crick (1980), in his biography, carries a picture of young Blair with his father in 1916 on leave from his duties in the Opium Department of the Government of India with his mother and sister, Marjorie. Here, father Blair looks rather awkward, stiff and strict, in an official-looking suit and cap. He sits separate from the others with their domestic intimacy. Shelden (1991) shows Mr Blair, in contrast, strolling down a road in Southwold during his retirement – a walking stick held elegantly before him. He is smiling and looking extremely relaxed and dapper. He's wearing a light suit, white polo-necked jumper, white shoes, a flowery buttonhole on his left lapel together with a colourfully displayed handkerchief in his top left blazer pocket and a lovely, large, white sun hat (with a fetching dark band) which bends enticingly over his forehead. D. J. Taylor examines the films of Southwold in the 1920s and 1930s shot by Barrett Jenkins and in one, dating 6 August 1928, he spots 'an elderly man wearing a Panama hat and a summer suit' taking a constitutional down the High Street. He writes: 'I have a hunch that this is Richard Walmesley Blair' (Taylor 2003: 236). Intriguingly, Orwell (perhaps echoing his father's fancy) regularly displays – in a rather dapper style – a handkerchief in his top jacket pocket: for instance, as Bernard Crick (1980) shows him with BBC colleagues, taking a cup of tea or typing in his Islington flat in 1945 and even while chiselling some wood in an office (books piled up in the background).

Another constant feature of Orwell's appearance is the pencil-thin moustache which he acquired while serving as an Imperial Policeman in Burma from 1922-1927 – and kept for the rest of

RICHARD LANCE KEEBLE

his life (Larkin 2004: 48-49). Perhaps it is a way of reminding himself constantly of the impact his service in Burma (where he grew to hate the imperial system of oppression) has had on the formation of his character and ideas. Or conversely it may reflect his acknowledgement of the importance of imperial service in the Blair family's history (Crick 1980: 45-47): a case, then, of Orwellian doublethink over his moustache. John Ross reports him as being 'meticulous about his moustache' even in the trenches as he fought alongside the Republican militia against Franco fascist soldiers in Spain 1937. 'He kept up appearances by shaving with wine which was more readily available than water' (Ross 2012: 206).

Orwell's clothes sense certainly appears to have both intrigued and annoyed Southwold residents when he returned to the Suffolk coastal town after his stint in Burma in the early 1930s. As the *Ipswich Star* points out in an article commemorating the 100 years since his birth in 1903, he is remembered in the town 'as a rather dishevelled unshaven figure, dressed in suits handmade by a local tailor that needed a good iron, a long scarf, and no hat – which in the 1930s was considered under-dressed … people felt rather sorry for his parents'.[1] As for shoes, they were a 'mini-obsession' for Orwell, according to Ross (ibid: 207): 'During World War II and after, shoes that fit him were simply unavailable in England and he tried to obtain them through friends with contacts in America. On a sight-seeing trip to Haworth parsonage, he was amazed at Charlotte Brontë's impossibly tiny boots.'

DRESSING DOWN AMONGST THE TRAMPS

John Sutherland focuses originally and entertainingly (with occasional lapses in bad taste) on the importance of smell in Orwell's writings (Sutherland 2016). In a similar way, it's possible to highlight, somewhat idiosyncratically perhaps, the importance of dress (and the opposite: nakedness) in the oeuvre. There are, for instance, three contrasting scenes in *Down and Out in Paris and London* (1980 [1933]) in which Blair pawns his clothes. In the first, he is desperate having not eaten nor smoked for a day-and-a-half and so goes to a Parisian pawnshop. But then he's surprised when offered just 70 francs for what he considers £10 worth of clothes. He decides against arguing. 'I now had no clothes except what I stood up in – the coat badly out at the elbow – an overcoat, moderately pawnable, and one spare shirt' (ibid: 23). Next, he goes to the pawnshop with two shabby overcoats and is surprised this time to receive as much as 50 francs. He reflects: 'It was almost as great a shock as the seventy francs had been the time before. I believe now that the clerk had mixed my number up with someone else's…' (ibid: 34).

When later Orwell moves from Paris to London, the crucial ritual involves the shedding of his clothes at a pawn shop and acquiring the gear of a tramp. Having handed over what he considers 'a quite good suit' he is given in exchange 'some dirty-looking rags' and a shilling (ibid: 70):

> The clothes were a coat, once dark brown, a pair of black dungaree trousers, a scarf and a cloth cap; I had kept my own shirt, socks and boots, and I had a comb and razor in my pocket. It gives me a very strange feeling to be wearing such clothes. I had worn bad enough things before but nothing at all like these; a gracelessness, a patina of antique filth, quite different from mere shabbiness. They were the sort of clothes you see on a bootlace seller, or a tramp. An hour later, in Lambeth, I saw a hang-dog man, obviously a tramp, coming towards me, and when I looked again it was myself, reflected in a shop window. The dirt was plastering my face already. Dirt is a great respecter of persons; it lets you alone when you are well dressed, but as soon as your collar is gone it flies towards you from all directions.

Orwell is fully aware of the power of clothes: he continues (ibid):

> My new clothes had put me instantly into a new world. Everyone's demeanour seemed to have changed abruptly. I helped a hawker pick up a barrow that he had upset. 'Thanks mate,' he said with a grin. No-one had called me mate before in my life – it was the clothes that had done it. For the first time I noticed, too, how the attitude of women varies with a man's clothes. When a badly dressed man passes them they shudder away from him with a quite frank movement of disgust, as though he were a dead cat. Clothes are powerful things. Dressed in a tramp's clothes it is very difficult, at any rate for the first day, not to feel that you are genuinely degraded.

JOHN BERGER ON HOW CLOTHES CAN NEVER DISGUISE CLASS

In his essay, 'The suit and the photograph', John Berger (1980) compares three photographs by the German August Sander (1876-1964). The first (dating from 1913) shows a group of peasants on the road heading for a dance. The second shows a group of peasant musicians displaying their instruments. In the third, a group of upper-class missionaries in 1931 are staring at the camera. Berger argues that the photographs demonstrate that there is no way in which any of the groups can disguise their class. Orwell, likewise, realises that the shabby clothes cannot help him disguise his class (emphasised by his old-Etonian accent). So while a tramp, he simply presents himself as a gentleman down on his luck – and the tramps accept him. As he writes in his short essay 'Clink' (Orwell 1980 [1932]: 380-386): 'The story I always tell [is] that my name is Edward Burton, and my parents kept a cake shop in Blythburgh, where I had been employed as a clerk in a draper's shop; that I had

had the sack for drunkenness and my parents, finally getting sick of my drunken habits, had turned me adrift' (ibid: 381). Biographer Gordon Bowker suggests the character Orwell invents 'sounds more Kipps than down-at-heel Bertie Wooster' (2003: 103)

In many ways, Orwell's London pawnshop ritual echoes that of Jack London in his searing exposé of East End poverty, *The People of the Abyss* (2004 [1903]), the book that had helped inspire Orwell on his tramping exploits. London describes removing his shoes and grey travelling suit and putting on the rags of a tramp. He continues:

> No sooner was I out on the streets than I was impressed by the difference in status effected by my clothes. All servility vanished from the demeanour of the common people with whom I came in contact. Presto! In the twinkling of an eye, so to say, I had become one of them. My frayed and out-at-elbows jacket was the badge and advertisement of my class, which was their class. It made me of like kind, and in place of the fawning and too respectful attention I had hitherto received, I now shared with them a comradeship (ibid).

DOWN-AND-OUTS: KEEPING UP APPEARANCES

Orwell's attention is often drawn to the down-and-outs' clothes. Of his Parisian friend Boris, he writes (Orwell 1980 [1933]: 27):

> All the clothes he now had left were one suit, with one shirt, collar and tie, a pair of shoes almost worn out and a pair of socks all holes. He also had an overcoat which he pawned in the last extremity. ... In spite of this Boris managed to keep a fairly smart appearance. He shaved without soap with a razor blade two months old, tied his tie so that the holes did not show and carefully stuffed the soles of his shoes with newspaper. Finally, when he was dressed, he produced an ink-bottle and inked the skin of his ankles where it showed through his socks. You would never have thought, when it was finished, that he had recently been sleeping under the Seine bridges.

And Boris is fully aware of the power of clothes. He comments: 'Appearance – appearance is everything, *mon ami*. Give me a new suit and I will borrow a thousand francs by dinner time. What a pity I did not buy a collar when we had money' (ibid: 38).

While later tramping in the East End, Orwell befriends Paddy: 'He was dressed, rather better than most tramps, in a tweed shooting jacket and a pair of old evening trousers with the braid still on them. Evidently, the braid figured in his mind as a lingering scrap of respectability, and he took care to sew it on again when it came loose. ... Nevertheless, one would have known him for a tramp a hundred yards away' (ibid: 88).

DRESSED FOR REVOLUTION

In December 1936, Orwell arrives in Barcelona and is so overwhelmed by the revolutionary fervour he witnesses that he immediately decides to fight alongside the Republicans against the fascist forces of General Franco. Indeed, he is lucky to escape with his life after he is shot by a sniper in the neck on 20 May. At the start of *Homage to Catalonia* (1962 [1938]: 7), his first-hand frontline account, he describes meeting an Italian militiaman at the Lenin Barracks. There are distinct homoerotic undertones to the writing (see Keeble 2019a) as Orwell dwells on his appearance: 'He was a tough-looking youth of twenty-five or -six, with reddish-yellow hair and powerful shoulders. ... Something in his face deeply moved me' (op cit: 7). The two exchange a few words. Orwell continues: 'As he went out he stepped across the room and gripped my hand very hard. Queer the affection you can feel for a stranger!' (ibid). Significantly, Orwell highlights a feature of his clothes, his 'peaked cap was pulled fiercely over one eye' (ibid) that seems to add to the Italian's allure.

Later on Orwell describes the overall situation in Barcelona – and he is keen to point out how the clothes he sees reflect the revolutionary spirit which so excites him:

> In outward appearance it was a town in which the wealthy classes had practically ceased to exist. Except for a small number of women and foreigners there were no 'well-dressed' people at all. Practically everyone wore rough working-class clothes or blue overalls or some variant of the militia uniform. All this was queer and moving. There was much in it that I did not understand, in some ways I did not even like it but I recognized it immediately as a state of affairs worth fighting for (ibid: 9).

At the end of the book, as Orwell and his new wife, Eileen, who has joined him at the frontline, prepare to escape from Spain as the communists ruthlessly suppress the Trotskyists and anarchists, the accompanying dampening of the revolutionary spirit is reflected in clothes. Now the safest thing is to look as 'bourgeois as possible' (ibid: 215). Orwell comments: 'By night we were criminals, but by day we were prosperous English visitors – that was our pose anyway. Even after a night in the open, a shave, a bath and a shoe-shine do wonders with your appearance' (ibid). On the train to France, Orwell reflects further on the significance of clothes:

> It was queer how everything had changed. Only six months ago, when the Anarchists still reigned, it was looking like a proletarian that made you respectable. On the way down from Perpignan to Cerbères, a French commercial traveller in my carriage had said to me in all solemnity: 'You mustn't go into Spain looking like that. Take off that collar and tie. They'll tear

RICHARD LANCE KEEBLE

them off you in Barcelona.' He was exaggerating but it showed how Catalonia was regarded. And at the frontier the Anarchist guards had turned back a smartly dressed Frenchman and his wife, solely – I think – because they looked too bourgeois. Now it was the other way about: to look bourgeois was the one salvation (ibid: 217).

Indeed, is it not also significant that the ruling pigs' ultimate betrayal of their former revolutionary ideals towards the end of *Animal Farm* (1976 [1945]) is reflected, in part, in their acceptance of the bourgeois dress codes of their former rulers? As Orwell writes: 'It did not seem strange when Napoleon [the leader] was seen strolling in the farmhouse garden with a pipe in his mouth – no, not even when the pigs took Mr Jones's clothes out of the wardrobes and put them on. Napoleon himself appearing in a black coat, ratcatcher breeches, and leather leggings, while his favourite sow appeared in the watered silk dress which Mrs Jones had been used to wear on Sundays' (ibid: 63-64).

HOW ORWELL'S BOHEMIAN DRESS CONFUSES THE SPOOKS

In August 1941, Orwell joined the Empire Department of the BBC as head of cultural programmes for India and south-east Asia. During his two-year, largely unhappy stint there, Orwell was closely watched by Special Branch (the source clearly being an employee of the BBC). This became clear after Orwell's Special Branch file (MEPO 38/69) and MI5 file (KV 2/2699) were released in 2005 and 2007 respectively (Smith 2013: 112). Intriguingly, Orwell's dress sense was highlighted in one report and may well have contributed to the spies' uncertainty over his political allegiances. For instance, a letter dated 20 January 1942 (file number 301/NWC/683), reports in detail on the office politics at the BBC and adds:

> Blair was at one time in the Burma Police … He was practically penniless when he found work with the BBC. This man has advanced communist views and several of his Indian friends say they have often seen him at communist meetings. He dresses in a bohemian fashion both at his office and in his leisure hours (Keeble 2012: 155).

A later note, dated 11 February 1942 (KV/2/2699) records Orwell's broadcasts to India and continues:

> ERIC BLAIR is better known as George ORWELL, author and journalist, he has been a bit of an anarchist in his day and in touch with extremist elements. But he has lately thrown in his lot with Victor Gollancz who as you probably know has severed all connection with the Communist Party. BLAIR has undoubtedly strong Left Wing views but he is a long way from orthodox Communism (ibid: 155).

The spooks are clearly flummoxed by Orwell's idiosyncratic brand of socialism – and even his mode of dress helps make it difficult for them to place him amongst any one particular faction of the left. As James Smith comments: 'If his bohemian dress sense was not suspicious enough, Orwell was also suggested to be part of a deeper conspiracy to place politically suspect individuals within the BBC' (Smith 2013: 122).

THE POLITICS OF DRESS AND CLOTHES RATIONING

In one of the 'London Letters' Orwell writes for the left-wing American journal, *Partisan Review*, during the war, Orwell tackles the politics of clothes rationing (see Newsinger 1999). On the surface, he says, the rationing appears to be an undemocratic measure since it hardly affects the rich who have large stocks of clothes already. 'Also the rationing only regulates the number of garments you can buy and has nothing to do with the price, so that you give up the same number of coupons for a hundred-guinea mink coat and a thirty-shilling waterproof' (Orwell 1970: 1942]: 269). However, it now seems rather the 'the thing' for people not in uniform to look shabby. Orwell continues:

> Evening dress has practically disappeared so far as men are concerned. Corduroy trousers and, in women, bare legs are on the increase. There hasn't yet been what one could call a revolutionary change in clothing but there may be one owing to the sheer necessity of cutting down wastage of cloth. The Board of Trade tinkers with the problem by, for example, suppressing the turn-ups of trouser ends but is already contemplating putting everyone into battledress (ibid).

THE PLEASURE OF THE DRESS AND MAKE-UP IN 'AS I PLEASE'

Between 1943 and 1947 Orwell contributed 80 'As I Please' columns to the leftist journal, *Tribune*, where he became literary editor after two unhappy years at the BBC. The subject matter was vast: writers and writing, critiques of the mainstream press, the war effort, language, personal reminiscence and experiences, media censorship and the promotion of free speech, the BBC, post-war reconstruction, racism/anti-racism/anti-semitism, the love of nature, socialism, the ruling classes, the handling of collaborators and so on. Orwell is, in effect, through his column defining a new kind of radical politics. It involves reducing the power of the press barons, facing up to racial intolerance, defending civil liberties. Yet it also incorporates an awareness of the power of language and propaganda, a celebration of the joys of nature and an acknowledgement of the cultural power of Christianity. Above all, in the face of the vast political, cultural, economic factors driving history, it recognises the extraordinary richness of the individual's experience – summed up in his idiosyncratic columns (Keeble 2000). And dress features in a number of intriguing ways in the columns.

RICHARD LANCE KEEBLE

For instance, in his 4 February 1944 column, Orwell – ever sensitive to the politics of dress and with both a droll wit and polemical vigour – returns to the Board of Trade ban on turned-up trouser ends (now lifted) with a socialistic point about the overall war effort. A tailor's advertisement hails the lifting of the ban as 'a first instalment of the freedom for which we are fighting'. Orwell comments: 'If we were really fighting for turn-up trouser-ends, I should be inclined to be pro-Axis. Turn-ups have no function except to collect dust, and no virtue except that when you clean them out you occasionally find a sixpence there' (Anderson 2006: 94). He continues:

> I would like to see clothes rationing continue till the moths have devoured the last dinner jacket and even the undertakers have shed their top hats. I would not mind seeing the whole nation in dyed battledress for five years if by that means one of the main breeding points of snobbery and envy could be eliminated. Clothes rationing was not conceived in a democratic spirit, but all the same it has had a democratising effect. If the poor are not much better dressed at least the rich are shabbier. And since no real structural change is occurring in our society, the mechanical levelling process that results from sheer scarcity is better than nothing (ibid).

On 28 April 1944, Orwell even confounds his feminist critics by following up the comments of Basil Henriques, chairman of the East London juvenile court, who has attacked girls of 14 for dressing and talking like those of 18 and 19 and putting 'filth and muck on their faces' (Anderson 2006: 132). The polymath Orwell (how much helped by his wife, Eileen O'Shaughnessy, it is hard to say) proceeds to offer a potted history of women's make-up – of all things.

> One of the big failures in human history has been the age-long attempt to stop women painting their faces. The philosophers of the Roman empire denounced the frivolity of the modern woman in almost the same terms as she is denounced today. In the fifteenth century, the church denounced the damnable habit of plucking the eyebrows. The English puritans, the Bolsheviks and the Nazis all attempted to discourage cosmetics, without success. In Victorian England, rouge was considered so disgraceful that it was usually sold under some other name, but it continued to be used.

Continuing with gusto on the same theme (and with no Google to assist him), Orwell suggests that many styles of dress, from the Elizabethan ruff to the Edwardian hobble skirt have been denounced from the pulpit, without success. 'In the 1920s, when skirts were at their shortest, the Pope decreed that women improperly dressed were not to be admitted to Catholic churches, but somehow feminine fashions remained unaffected. Hitler's "ideal woman", an exceedingly plain specimen in a mackintosh, was exhibited all over Germany and much of the rest of the world, but inspired few imitators' (ibid). And he ends this section of the column with a rousing defence of the girls: 'I prophesy that English girls will continue to "put filth and muck on their faces" in spite of Mr Henriques. Even in jail, it is said, the female prisoners redden their lips with the dye from the Post Office mail bags' (ibid).

Then, on 8 November 1946, he begins his column: 'Someone has just sent me a copy of an American fashion magazine which shall be nameless' (Orwell 1998 [1946]: 471). In fact, it was *Vogue* containing, amidst its many photographs of glamorous women, a short profile of Orwell – along with a photograph of him. Biographer Michael Shelden comments (1991: 455):

> Orwell must have felt a mixture of pride and embarrassment to see his personal life described in the breezy style of the *Vogue* correspondent: 'Nowadays, Orwell lives in a top-floor flat in London, with his twenty-odd-months-old son. The stuff around his rooms – a Burmese sword, a Spanish peasant lamp, the Staffordshire figures, show something of his foreign life and his strong English solidity. Educated at Eton, Orwell has since then had the kind of picaresque life that is so superb in English autobiographies.'

Orwell proceeds to deconstruct the magazine, noting : 'One striking thing when one looks at these pictures is the overbred, exhausted, even decadent style of beauty that now seems to be striven after. Nearly all of these women are immensely elongated.' On the prose style of the advertisements, he says it's 'an extraordinary mixture of sheer lushness with clipped and sometimes very expressive technical jargon'. And, typically, Orwell focuses on what's missing:

> A fairly diligent search through the magazine reveals two discreet allusions to grey hair, but if there is anywhere a direct mention of fatness or middle age I have not found it. Birth and death are not mentioned either: nor is work, except that a few recipes for breakfast dishes as given. The male sex enters directly or indirectly into perhaps one advertisement in twenty and photographs of dogs and kittens appear here and there. On only two pictures out of about three hundred, is a child represented (op cit: 472).

Alex Woloch actually highlights Orwell's habit – in his 'As I Please' columns and other essays – to focus on what we are 'liable to miss'. This, he suggests 'reveals a strange blankness, or emptiness, at the deliberate heart of Orwell's work' (2016: 23). Later, he describes this 'withholding at the center of his style' as the 'poetics of exclusion' (ibid: 67).

RICHARD LANCE KEEBLE

THE SYMBOLIC POWER OF NAKEDNESS

Just as clothes clearly fascinated Orwell, so did the absence of clothes – nakedness in its many manifestations. While reporting his trips to the London underworld of tramps and beggars, he dwells on their nakedness as symbolising their complete desexualised humiliation, subservience to the whims of the Tramp Major (who runs the doss-house with an iron hand), degradation and vulnerability. In the essay, 'Spike' which (as Eric Blair) he contributes to the left-wing *Adelphi* magazine, in April 1931, his depiction of the plight of the down-and-outs mixes both compassion and squeamishness (perhaps also reflecting the assumed response of his imaginary middle class audience) (Orwell 1970 [1941]). For instance, on the 'disgusting sight' in the bathroom, he writes

> All the indecent secrets of our underwear were exposed: the grime, the rents and patches, the bits of string doing duty for buttons, the layers upon layers of fragmentary garments, some of them mere collections of holes, held together by dirt. The room became a press of steaming nudity, the sweaty odours of the tramps competing with the sickly, sub-faecal stench native to the spike (ibid: 59-60)

As the men line up for the medical inspection, the narrator mixes cool observation with disgust (the adjectives piling on one after another):

> It was an instructive sight. We stood shivering naked to the waist in two long ranks in the passage. … No one can imagine, unless he has seen such a thing, what pot-bellied, degenerate curs we looked. Shock heads, hairy, crumpled faces, hollow chests, flat feet, sagging muscles – every kind of malformation and physical rottenness were there (ibid: 61).

Indeed, as Beci Dobbin stresses (2012: 68), Blair's tendency towards squeamishness betrays a distinct 'class specific sensibility'.

A similar scene is depicted in *Down and Out in Paris and London* after the tramps at the spike are told to strip and wait for their medical inspection:

> Naked and shivering, we lined up in the passage. You cannot conceive what ruinous, degenerate curs we looked, standing there in the merciless morning light. A tramp's clothes are bad, but they conceal far worse things; to see him as he really is, unmitigated, you must see him naked. Flat feet, pot bellies, hollow chests, sagging muscles – every kind of physical rottenness was there. Nearly everyone was under-nourished, and some clearly diseased two men were wearing trusses and as for the old mummy-like creatures of seventy-five, one

wondered how he could possibly make his daily march (Orwell 1980 [1933]: 87).

The experience of witnessing such sights of nudity clearly impacts considerably on Orwell and so he uses it as the basis for his 40-line, ten-stanza, rhyming poem 'A dressed man and a naked man' which is published by *Adelphi* in October 1933. Typically, Orwell is using a poem to reflect on a particularly important moment or feeling – and to play with language, tone and genre (here a witty narrative built around dialogue bursting with the vernacular). Outside a spike, one man is naked (how come?) and haggling with another over the price of his clothes. After the deal is sorted, the poem ends:

> A minute and they had changed about,
> And each had his desire;
> A dressed man and a naked man
> Stood by the kip-house fire.[2]

Intriguingly, there are echoes of the tramps' naked ugliness in Orwell's depiction of Winston Smith towards the end of his horrific torture ordeal in *Nineteen Eighty-Four*. Here, Winston's enforced nakedness symbolises his total humiliation and subservience to the power of the Party and the brutal O'Brien – and more generally the destruction of the human spirit by Big Brother totalitarianism. At this key moment in the narrative, Winston comes to represent nothing less than the 'last man' in his nakedness. Orwell writes:

> 'You are the last man,' said O'Brien. You are the guardian of the human spirit. You shall see yourself as you are. Take off your clothes' (Orwell ` 2000 [1949]: 310).[3]

So Winston proceeds to his remove 'filthy yellowish rags, just recognisable as remnants of underclothes' (ibid). And in a mirror a 'bowed, grey-coloured, skeleton thing' coming towards him is terrifying. The disgust Orwell felt towards the naked, disfigured tramps in the spike all those years ago is now captured in his portrayal of Winston:

> A forlorn, jailbird's face with a nobby forehead running back into a bald scalp, a crooked nose and battered looking cheekbones above which the eyes were fierce and watchful. The cheeks were seamed, the mouth had a drawn-in look. ... Except for his hands and a circle of his face, his body was grey all over with ancient, ingrained dirt. Here and there under the dirt there were the red scars of wounds and near the ankle the varicose ulcer was an inflamed mass of flakes of skin peeling off it. But the truly frightening thing was the emaciation of his body. The barrel of his ribs was as narrow as that of a skeleton:

RICHARD LANCE KEEBLE

the legs had shrunk so that the knees were thicker than the thighs. The curvature of the spine was astonishing. .. he was aware of his ugliness, his gracelessness (ibid: 311).

Some commentators have suggested that there is an element of merciless self-portraiture in this writing. As Jeffrey Meyers comments: 'Orwell's description of himself after the terrible effects of streptomycin [the drug brought specially over from the US to treat his TB] are close to his portrayal of Winston after his torture in the novel' (Meyers 2000: 286). For biographer Robert Colls, Orwell is evoking the image of Jews heading towards the Nazi gas chambers: 'We are all Jews now,' Colls writes (2013: 214). But for Dorian Lynskey, Winston is not really 'the last man'. 'He's just the latest symbolic victim to be broken down and rebuilt. ... There were Winstons before and there will be Winstons to come. Like Stalin's regime during the Great Terror, the Party doesn't fear heretics, it *needs* them, because its power is renewed by crushing them' (2019: 179-180, italics in the original).

O'Brien, secret friend turned torturer, next mocks him: 'I do not think there can be much pride left in you. You have been kicked and flogged and insulted, you have screamed with pain, you have rolled on the floor in your own blood and vomit. You have whimpered for mercy, you have betrayed everybody and everything. Can you think of single degradation that has not happened to you?' (ibid: 313). To which Winston replies: 'I have not betrayed Julia.' But then, later, as the rats move closer to his face in the Ministry of Love's Room 101, he screams out the ultimate betrayal: 'Do it to Julia! Do it to Julia! Not me! Julia! I don't care what you do to her. Tear her face off, strip her to the bones. Not me! Julia! Not me!' (ibid: 328).

NUDITY AND SEXUALITY

Nudity is also associated by Orwell, not surprisingly, with sexuality. In a letter from 1932 to Eleanor Jaques, one of the loves of his life during his time in Southwold after he returned from his stint as an Imperial Policeman in Burma (1922-1927), he talks of their walks along the River Blyth: '... that day in the wood along past Blythburgh Lodge – you remember that, & your nice white body in the dark green moss' (Taylor 2003: 125). This experience of sex *en plein air* seems to have impacted hugely on Orwell's imagination. In *Keep the Aspidistra Flying*, for instance, Gordon Comstock and Rosemary take the train and bus out to Farnham Common, have a meal and then head out into the open countryside with one clear intention – to make love. In a natural alcove by some bushes, he asks her to take her clothes off (Orwell 1976 [1936]: 666). And Orwell dwells on her nakedness:

> She had no shame before him. ... They spread her clothes out and made a sort of bed for her to lie on. Naked, she lay back,

her hands behind her head, her eyes shut, smiling slightly, as though she had considered everything and were at peace in her mind. For a long time he knelt and gazed at her body (ibid).

But alas, Gordon has not brought any contraceptives (his lack of money – which obsesses him – even interfering with his dreams of love-making) and so Rosemary rejects his advances.

And in *Nineteen Eighty-Four*, Winston Smith and Julia conduct a secret passionate affair. At the start of the novel, he sets his eyes on her at the Two Minutes Hate session, and her clothes seem to sum up her public persona (while, in fact, she is secretly promiscuous): 'She was a bold-looking girl of about twenty-seven with thick dark hair, a freckled face and swift, athletic movements. A narrow scarlet sash, emblem of the Junior Anti-Sex League, was wound several times round the waist of her overall, just tightly enough to bring out the shapeliness of her lips' (Orwell 2000 [1949]: 12).

Winston and Julia first make love *en plein air* (Orwell 2000 [1949]: 142-145) but are only naked together when they have sex in the room above Charrington's junk shop. Intriguingly, here the focus is more on Winston's nakedness than Julia's:

> They flung their clothes off and climbed into the huge mahogany bed. It was the first time that he had stripped himself naked in her presence. Until now he had been too much ashamed of his pale and meagre body, with the varicose veins standing out on his calves and the discoloured patch over his ankle (ibid: 165).

Charrington, however, turns out to be a member of the Thought Police – and Winston is hauled off to the Ministry of Love to be tortured. The question of whether Julia suffers a similar fate or is, instead, a Party member luring Winston into a trap is one of the many conundrums in the text (Keeble 2019b).

CONCLUSION: 'IT WAS THE CLOTHES THAT HAD DONE IT'

Orwell's life-long fascination with dress (and undress) has been largely missed by his biographers. This is perhaps not surprising: as Shahigha Bari comments in *The Secret Life of Clothes* (2019: 10): 'The ubiquity of clothes means that we can be careless of them too. We rarely think to take the things we wear and hold them up to the light, inspecting them as objects of intellectual enquiry.' Yet a close examination of Orwell's writings suggests that throughout his life the clothes he wore and he saw others wearing (whether on the streets of London while tramping, on the streets of revolutionary Barcelona or displayed in the pages of a flashy American women's magazine) were important to him and worth describing and commenting upon. Orwell was a complex man, contradictory in many aspects and certainly in his clothes sense – at one time shabby, at another time quite a dandy. Clothes, he also realised, were essentially markers of personality – and yet they could never disguise a person's class.

Conversely, states of undress also intrigue him: female nakedness always being associated with sexuality. Male nakedness, on the other hand, both fascinates and disgusts him – as his observations in the London spikes show. The system has rendered the down-and-outs nameless, 'inhumane' degenerates – reduced to animals by the Tramp Major 'who gave the tramps no more ceremony than sheep at the dipping pond, shoving them this way and that and shouting oaths in their faces' (1970 [1941]: 59). Blair/Orwell, in contrast, treats them with some measure of compassion, giving them names and distinct, contrasting personalities. In this context, their nakedness, which he describes in relentless detail, symbolises their humiliation, degradation and vulnerability.

After Orwell's first wife, Eileen O'Shaughnessy dies suddenly in 1945, aged just 39, his great friend David Astor, the *Observer* journalist and fellow old-Etonian, becomes probably the most important person in his life (Keeble 2012). I was lucky to interview Astor (one of the wealthiest men in Britain with a long history of ties to the intelligence services) just a year before he died in 2001. In the course of our two-hour conversation I asked him: 'Did you ever talk about your times at Eton with Orwell?' And Astor replied:

> Towards the end of his life, I had a son and I had to decide which school to send him to. I asked George: 'What do you think of Eton as a school?' And he said: 'I've got nothing against the education. I think it's very good. But they will have to change the school dress. I wouldn't let my son have to wear a tailcoat and make a fool of him' (Keeble 2014).

So right until near the very end, Orwell is a man acutely aware of the messages and ideas given out by clothes.

NOTES

[1] See https://www.ipswichstar.co.uk/home/george-orwell-great-but-a-bit-smelly-and-spiteful-about-southwold-1-4764498, accessed on 7 February 2020

[2] https://www.orwellfoundation.com/the-orwell-foundation/orwell/poetry/a-dressed-man-and-a-naked-man/

[3] Significantly, when Orwell first conceived of his dystopian novel 'some time between 1940 and the end of 1943' when Britain was seriously in danger of losing the war, his original title was *The Last Man in Europe* (Sutherland 2016: 226)

REFERENCES

Anderson, Paul (2006) *Orwell in* Tribune, London: Politico's

Bari, Shahidha (2019) *Dressed: The Secret Life of Clothes*, London: Jonathan Cape

Berger, John (1980) The suit and the photograph, in *About Looking*, London: Writers and Readers Publishing Cooperative pp 27-36

Bowker, Gordon (2003) *George Orwell*, London: Little, Brown

Colls, Robert (2013) *George Orwell: English Rebel*, Oxford: Oxford University Press

Crick, Bernard (1980) *George Orwell: A Life*, Harmondsworth, Middlesex: Penguin

Dobbin, Beci (2012) Orwell's squeamishness, Keeble, Richard Lance (ed.) *Orwell Today*, Bury St Edmunds: Abramis pp 62-76

Keeble, Richard Lance (2012) Orwell, *Nineteen Eighty-Four* and the spooks, Keeble, Richard Lance (ed.) *Orwell Today*, Bury St Edmunds; Abramis pp 151-163

Keeble, Richard Lance (2014) Exclusive: Orwell by his great friend David Astor, Orwell Society *Journal*, June, No. 4 pp 8-10

Keeble, Richard Lance (2019a) Beyond the dystopian gloom: Orwell and sexuality, Joseph, Sue and Keeble, Richard Lance (eds) *Sex and Journalism: Critical Global Perspectives*, London: Bite-Sized Books pp 88-96

Keeble, Richard Lance (2019b) *Nineteen Eighty-Four,* the secret state and the Julia conundrum, *George Orwell Studies*, Vol. 4, No. 1 pp 43-56

Kennedy, Maev (2017) George Orwell returns to loom over the BBC, *Guardian*, 7 November. Available online at https://www.theguardian.com/books/2017/nov/07/george-orwell-returns-to-loom-over-bbc, accessed on 5 September 2019

London, Jack (2004 [1903]) *The People of the Abyss*, Fairfield, IA: 1st World Library: Literary Society

Lynskey, Dorian (2019) *The Ministry of Truth: A Biography of George Orwell's 1984*, London: Picador

Meyers, Jeffrey (2000) *Orwell: Wintry Conscience of a Generation*, New York and London: W. W. Norton & Co.

Newsinger, John (1999) The American connection: George Orwell, 'Literary Trotskyism' and the New York intellectuals, *Labour History Review*, Vol. 64, No. 1 pp 23-43

Orwell, George (1980 [1933]) *Down and Out in Paris and London, George Orwell: Complete and Unabridged*, London: Secker and Warburg/Octopus pp 15-120

Orwell, George (1976 [1936]) *Keep the Aspidistra Flying*, London: Secker & Warburg/Octopus pp 573-737

Orwell, George (1976 [1945]) *Animal Farm*, London: Secker & Warburg/Octopus pp 13-66

Orwell, George (1962 [1937]) *Homage to Catalonia*, Harmondsworth, Middlesex: Penguin

Orwell, George (1970 [1941]) The Spike, Orwell, Sonia and Angus, Ian (eds) *The Collected Essays, Journalism and Letters of George Orwell, Vol. 1: An Age Like This 1920–1940,* Harmondsworth, Middlesex: Penguin Books pp 58-66; originally published in the *Adelphi*, April 1931

RICHARD LANCE KEEBLE

Orwell, George (1970 [1942]) London Letter to *Partisan Review*, 29 August, Orwell, Sonia and Angus, Ian (eds) *The Collected Essays, Journalism and Letters of George Orwell, Vol. 2: My Country Right or Left 1940-1943*, Harmondsworth, Middlesex: Penguin pp 265-272; originally published in November-December edition

Orwell, George (1998 [1946]) As I Please, Davison, Peter (ed.) Complete Works of George Orwell, Vol. 17: *Smothered Under Journalism, 1946*, London: Secker and Warburg pp 471–472; originally published in *Tribune*, 8 November

Orwell, George (2000 [1949]) *Nineteen Eighty-Four*, London: Penguin

Ross, John (2012) *Orwell's Cough: Diagnosing the Medical Maladies & Last Gasps of the Great Writers*, London: Oneworld

Shelden, Michael (1991) *Orwell: The Authorised Biography*, London: William Heinemann

Smith, James (2012) *British Writers and MI5 Surveillance 1930-1960*, Cambridge: Cambridge University Press

Sutherland, John (2016) *Orwell's Nose: A Pathological Biography*, London: Reaktion Books

Taylor, D. J. (2003) *Orwell: The Life*, London: Chatto & Windus

Woloch, Alex (2016) *Or Orwell: Writing and Democratic Socialism*, Massachusetts, London: Harvard University Press

NOTE ON THE CONTRIBUTOR

Richard Lance Keeble is Professor of Journalism at the University of Lincoln and Honorary Professor at Liverpool Hope University. His latest books are *Journalism Beyond Orwell* (Routledge, 2020) and *George Orwell, the Secret State and the Making of* Nineteen Eighty-Four (Abramis, 2020).

ARTICLE

What If He Had Lived ... or Waited?
George Orwell and Counterfactual Biography

John Rodden cannot resist pondering some of the 'what ifs' of Orwell's tragic, premature, untimely death. He argues: 'We need to see beyond our presentist bias and glimpse the origins, emergence and development of such a process – and never forget that Blair-Orwell was a man of his time.'

OVERTHROWING THE TYRANNY OF THE PRESENT

Few readers of Orwell ever pause to ask themselves how highly they would regard him if he had died little more than four years earlier – and thus never completed the searing, unforgettable *Nineteen Eighty-Four*. Or perhaps even to ask themselves if they would read him. When they eventually do ask themselves, as I have discovered, they concede that they might well consider him little more than a clever fabulist, indeed a one-book author. Many of the great essays would remain unwritten – and perhaps even those already published would be largely unknown, even possibly uncollected. There would be no *Complete Works of George Orwell* in twenty volumes. Possibly there would not even be a *Collected Works*.

It is easy to forget that the sensational impact of *Nineteen Eighty-Four* made all the rest of the story possible – the collection, publication and republication in edition after edition of his writings (even scraps of journalism, quickly jotted notes and forgettable juvenilia), the numerous radio and film and television adaptations and, of course, the blaring of his neologisms from *Nineteen Eighty-Four* itself (and the emergence of his surname as a fear-inducing proper adjective: 'Orwellian').

Let us review those last four or five years briefly, pausing to ask ourselves some 'what ifs'. Such reasoned conjectures are the stuff of counterfactual history; the resultant speculations liberate us momentarily from the tyranny of the present – the prison of 'presentism', as historians call it – by raising unasked questions and generating thought-provoking scenarios, all of which serves as rich food for thought. In doing so, it also reminds us that history is a parade of radically contingent events.

As if he somehow intuited that he was fated to die before the decade was out, the last five years of Orwell's life are packed with a concentrated dramatic power that is stupefying. Buffeted by one event after the next, with glorious peaks and death valleys, these fateful years bring his passionate pilgrimage to a crescendo.

FULFILMENT AND FINALE

The torrid march of events began to accelerate in mid-1944. In June, Eric and Eileen took home a three-week-boy, naming him Richard Horatio Blair, just days before their London home was hit by a V-1 bomb and destroyed. After staying a short spell in the country with the baby, they moved in September 1944 to a fifth-storey flat on Canonbury Road.

Orwell and Eileen didn't have much time to enjoy life together as a family. Orwell wanted to get to the front before the war ended. Through his friendship with David Astor, owner of the *Observer*, he was accredited as a war correspondent both by that paper and by the *Manchester Evening News*. In mid-February 1945, he flew to Paris to stay with other foreign correspondents at the Hotel Scribe. Travelling through liberated France and Allied-occupied Germany, he reported on wartime events for three months. Meanwhile, Eileen became ill and was told that her health condition necessitated a hysterectomy. On 29 March 1945, while undergoing the operation, she died at the age of 39. Orwell received the news by telegram in Paris and flew back to England. Soon he would begin what would turn out to be the final phase in his own shortened life.

As every student of Orwell knows, while working at the BBC, Orwell had begun writing what would become his breakthrough book, *Animal Farm*. He finished the book, a bitter parody of the Russian Revolution, in February 1944 and circulated it among London publishers for more than a year without success. No press wanted to publish a book critical of a wartime ally and thereby potentially disrupt the war effort and even endanger the campaign against Nazi Germany. Finally, Secker and Warburg accepted *Animal Farm*, but wartime paper shortages and other delays postponed its release (in a modest edition of 4,500 copies) until 17 August 1945, just days after the official end of World War Two. Selling 140,000 copies in Britain by the year's close, *Animal Farm* was a stunning success. A year later it became a runaway bestseller in the United States, where it was chosen as the Book-of-the-Month Club selection for September 1946. During the next four years, *Animal Farm* sold a half-million copies in the United States alone. Orwell was financially secure for the rest of his life.

Alas, it was all too late to save him. Orwell's tuberculosis flared up once again, this time more seriously. Still, he used the money from *Animal Farm* to rent a farm, Barnhill, on the island of Jura, part of the Inner Hebrides, off the west coast of Scotland. He had grown to dislike London and wanted a quiet place to raise his son and write. He went to Barnhill for the first time in the spring of 1946, staying for four months to make the house habitable. He would return to London for a time, but after 1946 Barnhill was his formal residence. He loved its isolation, its surprisingly mild climate – the Gulf Stream flowed close by – and its fishing. His health nevertheless deteriorated steadily. Beginning in December 1947 Orwell spent seven months in Hairmyres Hospital near Glasgow coping with a bout of tuberculosis. A second, more serious episode occurred in January 1949, after which Orwell spent eight months in the Cotswold Sanatorium in Gloucestershire trying to recover. But the damage to his lungs was too far advanced. He was transferred to University College Hospital, London, on 3 September 1949, just weeks after the June publication of his last book, his towering and terrifying masterpiece, *Nineteen Eighty-Four.*

Between bouts of illness, he had laboured over the manuscript for three years, even typing a draft himself in Barnhill when he could not secure a secretary. Finally published in June 1949 in England and the United States – where it was the Book-of-the-Month Club choice for July – it received glowing reviews and elicited comparisons between its author and utopian satirists ranging from Swift to Dostoyevsky, Shaw and Wells.

Desperate for a companion who would rejuvenate him and share his life, Orwell had been searching for a wife since Eileen's death. He proposed to four young women, possibly more, but was rejected. On 13 October 1949, however, he married Sonia Brownell, 29, a secretary at his friend Cyril Connolly's literary magazine *Horizon*. Three months later, on 21 January 1950, Orwell died of pulmonary tuberculosis at the age of 46 years and seven months.

THE WHAT-IFS…

The 'what ifs' of Orwell's tragic, premature, untimely death have been irresistible to biographers, critics and avid readers of Orwell:

- What if Orwell had not been so impatient to complete *Nineteen Eighty-Four*?
- What if he had not overstrained himself to produce a cleanly typed version of the manuscript in the winter of 1948-1949 on the secluded island of Jura in the Scottish Hebrides?
- What if he had simply traveled to London during that winter and worked there with a typist?

JOHN RODDEN

- What if he had waited patiently on Jura until the following summer, when it is likely that a typist would have been willing to spend several weeks with him there? His publisher and friends could find no secretary to travel to and reside on Jura to type the book. So he rashly decided to do the job himself – and suffered on its completion his last and fatal hemorrhage of the lungs, a development that landed him in sanatoria in Scotland and later in London, from which he never emerged.

It warrants emphasis that not only his publisher Fred Warburg, but also several friends of Orwell canvassed London to find a typist willing to travel to Jura and type the manuscript there. All efforts failed. Certainly the tubercular Orwell was well aware that undertaking the task of typing the manuscript himself might shatter his fragile health completely – and thus kill him.

Yet had he not for years been heedless of his physical well-being? Had he not almost defiantly been risking his life for decades? Indeed, his decisions both to fight in Spain and semi-retire in remote Jura far from any medical facility typified his reckless disregard for his failing health. To complete *Nineteen Eighty-Four,* his *chef d'oeuvre* and (perhaps sole) claim to fame, might have entailed sacrificing the man Blair for the writer Orwell.

Yet had not that very trade-off been in progress for two decades? If he intuited that such a price would have to be paid, he could at least console himself with the fantasy that he had exited in triumph and martyred himself for a great cause: the possibility that Blair's death would grant Orwell life, perhaps even literary immortality.

Can one conclude, as does a sympathetic reader of Edgar Allan Poe, who also suffered a lifetime of debilitating illness and died young (aged just 40), that Orwell 'paid dearly for immortality, gave his whole life to attain it. But in his terms it was probably worth the cost'?[1]

Finis coronat opus? Did 'the end crown the work'? Or just spawn the 'Work' (i.e., the bogeyman behemoth, *Nineteen Eighty-Four*)? E. M. Forster told BBC Radio listeners just months after Orwell's death: '*Nineteen Eighty-Four* crowned his work, and it is understandably a crown of thorns.'

That was a widespread view after Orwell's death, and Forster's judgment helped to reinforce it. Nonetheless, it needs emphasis that Blair-Orwell did not want to die. He still wanted to live, passionately so. He had just remarried, had new literary projects underway and had still others in mind. He yearned both to live and to complete what might become his lasting memorial. His death was a misfortune, not a conscious, affirmed act of will.

Nineteen Eighty-Four did not represent Orwell's deliberate 'parting testament', I believe, just his last book.

… AND IF HE HAD WAITED…

On the other hand, let us reframe these questions and shift our attention from the life to the afterlife.

- What if he had delayed completing *Nineteen Eighty-Four* until he found a London secretary?
- What if his health had not broken down from the exertion and exhaustion of pushing himself to type *Nineteen Eighty-Four?*
- What if he had relocated to London and been under constant medical care as he supervised a typist's progress on the manuscript?[2]
- What if the novel had appeared in print even just a year later rather than detonating on the cultural front just as the Cold War was approaching its height in June 1949 – only a dozen weeks before the explosion of the Soviet Union's first atomic bomb in August 1949?

If any of these scenarios had come to pass, perhaps both Orwell and the novel never would have become so famous and controversial. After all, the Cold War would have already entered an even deeper phase by mid-1950, with both the Red Scare and McCarthyism fully underway in the United States since February 1950. If so, perhaps its impact as the 'prophetic' work of a dying 'visionary' might have been much attenuated (or even seemed anticlimactic).

For its publication date would then have followed – rather than preceded and 'forecast' – the alarming events of fall 1949 to spring 1950: President Harry Truman's reluctant announcement on 23 September of the Soviet Union's successful atomic test; the victorious Mao Zedong's proclamation forming a communist People's Republic of China on 1 October; the perjury conviction of Alger Hiss, a former State Department official turned Soviet agent, on 21 January (Orwell's last day); émigré German scientist Klaus Fuchs's confession that he had spied for the Soviet Union as a researcher for the Manhattan Project on 24 January; Truman's declaration that the United States would build a 'super-bomb' (later known as a thermonuclear or 'hydrogen' bomb) on 31 January; Wisconsin junior senator Joseph McCarthy's incendiary speech denouncing 'the traitorous actions' of those like Hiss with 'the finest jobs in government' on 5 February; and on and on, arguably culminating in the outbreak of a new war, one that would soon engulf the United States, the Soviet Union and China, when North Korea invaded South Korea on 25 June, roughly a year after *Nineteen Eighty-Four's* release (and, in a fittingly ironic twist, Orwell's birthday).

JOHN RODDEN

Yet if such events had intervened, perhaps *Nineteen Eighty-Four* would never have exploded so thunderously on the cultural front. Perhaps Orwell's incredible posthumous fame would never have developed or the disputes about his legacy never have arisen. Perhaps Clio would have never secured the alchemical raw materials – that is, the requisite admixture of historical events – out of which she would brew the all-too-human Orwell into the mythic, monstrous 'Orwell'. Was this the crafty handicraft of the Hegelian cunning of reason in History? And yet still again, even if we grant that he remained on Jura and typed the novel himself . . .

- What if he had not received such a strong dose (i.e., an overdose, with awful side effects) of streptomycin, the new miracle drug for tuberculosis that had been smuggled in for him from the United States?

- What if his doctors (among them Andrew Morland, who had also handled the case of D. H. Lawrence) had experimented with the doses that they administered to Orwell?[3]

- What if he had recovered – or even just become 'a good chronic' (in Morland's phrase) and survived a few more years?

If he had lived … then perhaps the 'Orwellian' ideological graffiti smeared by decades of screeching sound bites and scarifying headlines, as it were, across Eric Blair's headstone and George Orwell's heritage – which has both defaced and served to conflate Blair/Orwell and 'Orwell' – would never have occurred, since Orwell would have been able to contest claims to his name and novel. Irony of ironies: the side effects Orwell suffered while being treated with streptomycin were so horrible that he stopped taking it and donated his unused medicine to two tuberculosis victims, both of whom recovered under the reduced dosages.

UNSAINTLY GEORGE

George Orwell – or rather 'Eric Blair' – was buried at Sutton Courtenay, then in Berkshire, on 26 January 1950. The latter name not only was engraved on his tombstone ('Here Lies Eric Blair,' it reads), but was also the one he used in legal circumstances all his life. (Asked once if he had ever considered changing his name officially, he replied waggishly: 'Ah yes, but then I'd have to write under a different name, you see.' Oddly enough, however, Sonia Brownell used the married name 'Orwell'.)

Thus Eric Blair remained the identity of his personal life, whereas Orwell became the literary personality. And so, in a final irony, this incarnated *nom de plume* – the only fully rounded, three-dimensional character that the novelist ever created – would live on in his books. And he would do so not just in a leather-bound *Collected Works* that Blair had fantasised as an adolescent would be published, but in a magisterial *Complete Works* about which he never remotely dreamed. Nor could he even have dared to fantasise that his last book might become his *monumentum aere perennius*, exist in dozens of languages and be found in virtually every city throughout the globe. No, the name 'George Orwell' would not need to be etched in stone.[4]

So ended his life. His remarkable and utterly unprecedented afterlife thereupon commenced. Just a word about it here is apposite. Let it be understood that Eric Blair, aka George Orwell, the man of clay exalted today as 'St. George' Orwell – the radiant literary personality apotheosised by acclamation and canonised in curricula – was no 'saint'. Perhaps he was not even the 'virtuous man' whom Lionel Trilling memorialised or the 'social saint' honoured by John Atkins. He was a great writer, a decent man, and reportedly a good and faithful friend. At the same time, this quixotic, adamantly unsainted man had an anti-Semitic streak, an ambivalence toward homosexuals and a dislike of feminism. He led a somewhat conflicted personal life, as his numerous infidelities during his marriage to Eileen attest. He was a mortal like all of us, with all of the foibles and flaws of a fallible human being.

'Saints should always be judged guilty until they are proven innocent,' wrote Orwell just a year before his death in 'Reflections on Gandhi'. Orwell certainly would have applied that standard first and foremost to himself if the thought (which would have seemed to him bizarre) had ever crossed his mind that he might someday be exalted as an exemplar of virtue. He would have entered a plea of *nolo contendere* if his own personal life had ever come under the inquisitional gaze of the Thought (and Behavioural) Police. Taking him at his own word, we should accept his plea of 'guilty'.

The task for us readers in the twenty-first century is neither to prostrate ourselves before a canonical 'St George' nor to deface his gravesite. Rather, it is to read his often challenging, sometimes half-baked writings closely, distinguish his fine work from his 'good bad books' and occasional tripe, and aim to see his life clearly and see it whole. At his best, he himself did exactly that; let his own example as a critic and intellectual inspire us by its virtues and both enlighten and restrain us by its failings.

All this should remind us that Eric Blair became George Orwell, just as Orwell became 'Orwell'. We need to see beyond our presentist bias and glimpse the origins, emergence and development of such a process – and never forget that Blair-Orwell was a man of his time and led a writer's life, a London literary life of the 1930s and 1940s filled with personal friendships and rivalries, encounters with book publishers and magazine editors, marriages and love affairs, travails with physical health, and the upheavals of war and family tragedy.

JOHN RODDEN

He was no 'classic' Author dwelling in a literary firmament of canonised 'stars', no 'monument' of *Collected Works* (let alone multivolume *Complete Works*), no gargantuan 'Orwell' bestriding the twentieth century. He became all this – and that 'becoming' was to no small degree *our* doing.

Today only the texts remain. But the texts alone are inevitably misread if we remain inattentive to the daily round of the man's material existence, the dense texture of the writer's life experience from which they arose. Absent this context, the texts are engorged by 'Orwell' – the canonical 'St. George' – and are willy-nilly exalted into classics ascribed to a monumental Figure rocketed into the celestial statusphere – as if they and their reception (and production and distribution) somehow exist apart from the social processes of reputation-building and canon formation; indeed, as if they exist (and have always existed) above and beyond the quotidian realities of the life of the man who composed them.

All this is as well to remind us – myself above all – of a dictum I first expressed in the opening line of my first study of Orwell a decade ago: 'Reputations are made, not born.'

NOTES

[1] The observation about Poe is by Philip Van Doren Stern, cited in J. R. Hammond, *A George Orwell Chronology* (London: Palgrave, 2000 xi–xii). For Forster's BBC address, see *The Listener*, 2 November 1950, reprinted in E. M. Forster, *Two Cheers for Democracy* (London: Abingdon, 1951). Forster was discussing Orwell's dystopia and its satiric themes, not his life or death, let alone the possibility of his (half-deliberate?) self-martyrdom

[2] For that matter, what if his brother-in-law, Laurence O'Shaughnessy (Eileen's brother, also called 'Eric' by family members) – a brilliant doctor specialising in the treatment of tuberculosis – had not died during the Dunkirk evacuation in May 1940. (He was in a house that received a direct hit from German bombers.) If he had lived … so too may have Orwell

[3] Yes, and therefore, why not entertain other, equally plausible counterfactual scenarios earlier in Orwell's adventuresome, perhaps reckless life. Just one example here: what if, in May 1937, the Falangist bullet had not missed his carotid artery by millimeters? Or if weeks later the manhunt by the Spanish police (under orders from Stalin's NKVD) to capture and execute him had succeeded (as it did with Orwell's colleague, the POUM leader Andrés Nin)? Dead at the age of 33, Orwell would have left not just his political fantasias but even *Homage to Catalonia* and all his greatest essays forever unwritten. Then George Orwell would have gone down the memory hole just as surely as have most of his friends and colleagues – and no less justifiably

[4] Admittedly, as a mere toddler of 70, *Nineteen Eighty-Four* has a long, long way to go before Orwell can echo Horace's proud boast. *Exegi monumentum aere perennius* declares the poet as he closes the first three books of his *Odes* (III, 30). 'I have erected a monument more lasting than bronze.' Horace has often been mocked for his braggadocio. Given that his *Odes* are well past 2K on the endurance clock and still widely quoted, however, his boast doesn't sound so empty

NOTE ON THE CONTRIBUTOR

John Rodden has written several books on the work and heritage of George Orwell, including *George Orwell, Life and Letters, Legend and Legacy*, just published by Princeton University Press.

ARTICLE

RE-EVALUATION

Stansky and Abrahams:
Orwell's First Biographers

Darcy Moore examines the special contribution to Orwell Studies made by American academics Peter Stansky and William Abrahams in their pioneering biographies. He concludes that, above all, their works serve to emphasise 'the seminal importance of Orwell's early life to the understanding of his literary development'.

> I request that no memorial service be held for me after my death and that no biography of me shall be written **(Eric Blair, 18 January 1950)**.
>
> Perhaps Orwell was right to resist the idea of a biography and one might regret helping to start the onslaught. But it was bound to happen **(Peter Stansky, 2003)**.

George Orwell's last book review, of *Dickens: His Character, Comedy and Career*, by Hesketh Pearson, has a characteristically authoritative opening sentence: 'Literary men are apt to make poor subjects for biography, especially when, as in the case of Dickens, their careers are successful from the start' (Orwell 1998 [1949-1950]: 113). Orwell thought autobiography even more problematic, suggesting it should only be trusted when revealing something disgraceful as a 'man who gives a good account of himself is probably lying, since any life when viewed from the inside is simply a series of defeats' (Orwell 1998 [1943-1944]: 223-224). Friends and acquaintances (Atkins 1971; Brander 1954; Heppenstall 1960; Hollis 1956; Hopkinson 1953; Potts 1960; Rees 1961 and Woodcock 1967) sidestepped the thorny issue of Orwell's request for no biography, written three days before his death, by restricting their publications to literary criticism and memoirs. Ironically, by his own definition, Orwell was not a 'poor subject' for biographers and had unwittingly created a heavy burden for his widow, Sonia Brownell, until her own death in the year the first *full* biography was finally published (Orwell 1998 [1949-1950]: 308).

The first biographies into print, *The Unknown Orwell* (1972) and *Orwell: The Transformation* (1979) by Peter Stansky and William

Abrahams, covered the period 1903-1937 and arguably shaped the scholarly discourse more than is generally acknowledged. Their thesis, to understand George Orwell one must know Eric Blair, explored early influences on the writer's literary and intellectual development. Brownell, who used the pseudonym Orwell rather than Blair, even after re-marrying, had previously failed to convince Richard Ellmann (who had written biographies of Yeats, Joyce and Wilde) to take on the task and Malcolm Muggeridge, who agreed, failed to produce one (ibid: 308). The unauthorised publication of *The Unknown Orwell* led to Bernard Crick being granted unrestricted access to the Orwell Archive at University College London and commissioned to produce an official biography. Brownell was to become bitterly disappointed with the dry, overly political and (as she considered) unsympathetic representation of her late husband that Crick, a political theorist and democratic socialist, eventually published in 1980 (Meyers 2000: 317). More than a decade elapsed before Michael Shelden's, *Orwell: The Authorised Biography* (1991) was released. This was followed by Jeffrey Meyers (2000) with Gordon Bowker and D. J. Taylor both publishing biographies during the centenary of Orwell's birth in 2003.

RE-EVALUATION

Stansky and Abrahams were not granted the authority to quote from the standard published works or materials stored in the Orwell Archive. Stansky believes that Sonia Brownell, with whom he and Abrahams had a boozy lunch in London during the summer of 1963, was originally very receptive to their research interests suggesting several interviewees, including Orwell's youngest sister, Avril Dunn (Cushman and Rodden 2004: 191-192). Stansky and Abrahams stressed to Brownell that their Orwellian research was part of a larger project into Julian Bell, Stephen Spender and John Cornford who, along with Orwell, were in Spain during the civil war (1936-1937). Sonia's relaxed attitude – together with copyright law – had certainly changed by 1967. Stansky explains that Brownell would permit the use of 'the archive only if we would show her the manuscript' and seek 'total approval' (ibid: 192). They refused.

There was, however, no compelling legal reason not to write a biography and Richard Rees, Orwell's friend and co-literary executor, encouraged them to do so (Rodden 2009: 149). Understandably, one of the major criticisms levelled at the two biographies, even by sympathetic commentators, is that the legal reality of not being able to use quotations meant the two volumes lacked 'Orwell's voice' (Shelden 1991: 6; Rodden 2009: 150). This impacted less on the biographers than one would imagine due to the quality of both the writing and original research. They interviewed many who had known Orwell intimately and Stansky felt 'it didn't hurt us with others that we were on bad terms with Sonia' as she was disliked by many relatives and friends (Cushman and Rodden 2004: 192).

Ironically, as *The Collected Essays, Journalism and Letters of George Orwell*, edited by Ian Angus and Sonia Orwell, was published in 1968, it made Orwell's written legacy available to the researchers while they worked on their manuscript (ibid: 187). It is important to note this ground-breaking collection – four substantial volumes of carefully selected and edited non-fiction – was to reveal very little of the period before the publication of Orwell's first book, *Down and Out in Paris and London* (1933). Orwell himself had written: 'I do not think one can assess a writer's motives without knowing something of his early development' (Orwell 1998 [1946]: 318). Stansky and Abrahams had amassed, in their pioneering work, 'a wealth of information to support the little-known fact that Blair was quite a literary man with no political orientation before he became George Orwell' when readers, more than two decades after his death, were 'at last fully introduced to Eric Blair' (Rodden 2009: 149-150).

RECEPTION

The Unknown Orwell was widely and mostly positively reviewed on publication, as was *Orwell: The Transformation* (Jellinek 1972; Connolly 1972; Beadle 1973; Milton 1980; Winegarten 1980). There were some dissenters who mostly highlighted the 'impossibility' of writing a biography without the support of those who managed the subject's literary estate (Sedgwick 1972; Spender 1972; Hynes 1980). Sonia Orwell took the unusual step of writing a letter expressing dismay at what she felt was a misinterpretation of Orwell's 'character' and literary figures who had known her late husband waded into the debate. Stephen Spender, described as a poet of the 'pansy Left' by Orwell in the 1930s (he later apologised), wrote:

> Just as I sat down to write this article, a letter appeared in *The Times Literary Supplement* (October 13) from Orwell's widow, Sonia Orwell, stating that *The Unknown Orwell* by Peter Stansky and William Abrahams contains 'mistakes and inaccuracies' and misinterprets Orwell's character, and that it was written without her cooperation (with the result that the authors were not permitted to see important documents at University College London, which are in her trust).

Spender's review gives the impression of being written with Orwell's widow peering over his shoulder. He struggled with the 'Blair-Orwell dichotomy' believing they 'drive the thesis too hard' making 'the reader think that Orwell was a kind of split personality divided into a Jekyll-and-Hyde of Blair-and-Orwell'. However, Spender acknowledges that *The Unknown Orwell* is 'neither gossipy nor malicious' and 'it is difficult to think that seeing the withheld material would have substantially altered their views' (Spender 1972).

Cyril Connolly, Orwell's lifelong friend, in a lengthy and positive review, felt differently:

> Where I think these two collaborators have succeeded is in facing up to the difficult problem of not only 'how' but 'why' Eric Blair with his shabby-genteel background and Establishment education just right for the higher branches of the civil service threw it all up to become the proletarian champion, George Orwell. 'But it was not the name that mattered, it was the self, the essential second self which had been set free' (Connolly 1972).

Stansky and Abrahams interviewed Connolly several times for their Orwell biographies and while researching an earlier book, *Journey to the Frontier: Two Roads to the Spanish Civil War* (1966). Connolly was uniquely placed intellectually, historically and socially to understand Blair, the man who was to become Orwell. He knew most of Orwell's literary friends and, significantly, was schooled with Eric Blair at St Cyprian's prep school and later at Eton. Coincidentally, Connolly had been in Paris at the same time as Blair in the late 1920s, just a few streets from each other, without ever knowing it (Lewis 2012). They both corresponded about their experience in Spain during the civil war and the challenges of publishing reportage, like *Homage to Catalonia* (1937). Orwell had been introduced to Sonia Brownell by Connolly while she worked as his assistant on *Horizon*, a journal that published many of Orwell's finest essays during the 1940s. Connolly's *Enemies of Promise* (1938) is unique among the memoirs that refer to Orwell in that it was written before the fame generated by the publication of *Animal Farm* (1945) and *Nineteen Eighty-Four* (1949). Stansky and Abrahams must have greatly enjoyed reading his review.

Another friend, Arthur Koestler, who was very positive about Stansky and Abrahams's work, expressed his disappointment with Crick's biography of Orwell, believing it to be a 'blurred portrait' (Koestler 1980). Rayner Heppenstall, in agreement with Koestler, employed the same adjective, 'blurred', in his review (Heppenstall 1981). Bernard Crick, in a lecture 'On the Difficulties of Writing Biography in General and of Orwell's in Particular', unconvincingly addresses the criticisms made of his work, especially by Koestler and other friends who, he felt, failed to understand why he was so 'explicitly sceptical of the concept of character' (Crick 1989: 125). In the same lecture, Crick manages to avoid mentioning Stansky and Abrahams (which is strange considering the topic and how many biographies were published at the time) except to say that they had 'found a lady whom Orwell had told that he never saw a hanging' (ibid: 132) and that by their second volume they had decided to drop the 'Eric Blair/George Orwell disjunction' (ibid: 127). Crick appears careless in making such a judgment as the textual evidence reveals this is incorrect. Part One is titled 'Beginning as Orwell' and Part Three 'The End of Blair' (Stansky and Abrahams 1979: 1, 147). On the opening page, 'the difference between being Blair and being Orwell' is slight and the concluding page tells the reader that Blair was able to 'find his way as an artist … he became George Orwell' (ibid: 3, 285).

Crick felt strongly that it was not possible to make a 'proper assessment of Orwell until the so-called *Collected Essays, Journalism and Letters* of 1968 appeared' which, of course, Stansky and Abrahams were not permitted to quote from in their work but were able use for their research. Crick does not mention that these four volumes only include one personal letter that predates 1930 (*CEJL* Vol. 1 1968) which meant that the interviews conducted with those who knew Blair, before his pseudonym was born, were invaluable to understanding the first half of his life. Crick makes an important point that those who knew Orwell had their memories 'contaminated' by his posthumous fame. He cites Avril Dunn, Orwell's youngest sister, as an example, valuing her earliest interviews with the BBC in the 1950s highly compared to later ones (Crick 1989: 131). It is worth noting that Stansky and Abrahams had the advantage of interviewing many of those who knew Orwell best before a procession of biographers made their rounds (e.g. Crick 1992 [1980]; Wadhams 1984; Shelden 1991; Meyers 2000; Bowker 2003; Taylor 2003).

Other Orwell biographers criticised Stansky and Abrahams's two volumes, sometimes perceptively but occasionally misunderstanding what the vast majority of readers found satisfying in a biography. Meyers – the first biographer to publish after the release of the comprehensive twenty-volume, *The Complete Works of George Orwell* (1998) edited by Peter Davison – was particularly scathing in his analysis. His main charge is that the Blair-Orwell dichotomy is too simplistic and not even original. This theme, he says, suggested to the authors by Richard Rees, had already been explored by Tosco Fyvel, in his 1959 essay, 'George Orwell and Eric Blair' and in Keith Alldritt's book, *The Making of George Orwell*, a decade later (Meyers 2010: 203). Stansky and Abrahams, in their foreword, clearly outlined how this first volume came to be written and quoted Rees's offhand remark, from 1967: 'If you want to understand Orwell, you have to understand Blair …and to understand Blair – well there's your book' (Stansky and Abrahams 1972: xiv). Considering that the first chapter of Raymond Williams's *Orwell* is titled 'Blair into Orwell' (Williams 1971: 7), it is unlikely that Stansky and Abrahams were under any illusion that this had not yet been considered as a sensible approach to framing their subject's literary and artistic development.

Meyers, with a backhanded compliment, says the most 'interesting' section of the biography is on Burma, 'although the authors have not found any new letters ... and did not visit the country' (Meyers 2010: 204). Crick also notes that Stansky and Abrahams are 'excellent' on Burma having the advantage of being able to 'interview or correspond with several of Orwell's contemporaries who were dead by the time I started work' (Crick 1992: 616). Stansky was fortunate in that he discovered a close friend's father had worked for Burmah Oil and was a member of the Rangoon Club. Mr Cargill Thompson was able to assist with identifying members of the club who were police officers at the same time as Orwell. Many replied to letters Stansky wrote to them care of the India Office in London which greatly assisted with writing this section of the book (Stansky 2019). Due to the lack of primary sources for this period of Orwell's life (1922-1927), Crick, Shelden, Bowker and Taylor make considerable use of this information in their own biographies. My own research experience confirms how seminal *The Unknown Orwell* is for understanding Eric Blair's experience of Burma (Moore 2018).

RE-EVALUATION

Of course, biographers have always castigated the works that preceded (or followed) their own. Shelden (1991: 7) and Crick (1992: 582-606) traded blows. Stansky described Bowker (2003) as having a 'rather cavalier attitude to facts' and along with Taylor (2003) having 'too much emphasis' on Orwell as a 'philanderer' (Stansky 2003). Stansky relates an anecdote from an Orwell conference he attended, at the Library of Congress in 1984, where Jeffrey Meyers and Bernard Crick were also scheduled to speak. Considering both had made negative comments on his work, Stansky decided not to initiate conversation with either. Bernard Crick came up to him, though, and broke the ice rather wickedly: 'Shall we bury our hatchets (dramatic pause) in Jeffrey Meyers's skull?' (Stansky 2019).

ON READING STANSKY AND ABRAHAMS TODAY

The first biography of Orwell I read, in the year it was published, was by Michael Shelden (1991). Biographies by Crick, Bowker, Taylor and Colls followed. I even worked my way through Davison's magisterial *Complete Works* before finally getting around to reading Stansky and Abrahams's two volumes of biography. I had assumed their early diptych would be outdated, especially as the authors had limited archival access and were not authorised to employ quotations but I did not find this to be the case at all. In fact, they were captivating. The thrust of their argument – to know Orwell one must understand Blair – was not only convincing, it just seemed obviously correct. Not all reviewers, scholars or other biographers agreed with this sentiment, but the criticisms of these early biographies seem overblown when reading them today.

Having read obsessively widely about Orwell, I recognised factual errors, made almost fifty years ago in this pioneering work but these did not detract from the literary pleasure both volumes provided. Indeed, it was amazing just how many insights and how much information both books, castigated for their 'thinness' (Meyers 2010: 203), contained. I *re-read* them by *listening* to the dulcet tones of Tim Dalgleish narrate the audiobook, now available at *audible.com.au*, the Amazon-owned website where both volumes are combined into one audio download. My only real criticism of the production is that some basic errors have not been corrected; for example, Eric Blair did not return to England with his mother aged four (apparently the source of the misinformation was Avril Dunn's faulty memory). I searched for the other biographies – by Bowker, Taylor, Shelden, Meyers and Crick – but they were not available for digital download (although there is an excellent reading of Shelden's biography available on compact disc). A new generation of readers will continue to enjoy the work of Orwell's first biographers via a different medium which will extend the reach and life of the original print publications.

Particularly memorable sections for me in the two volumes included those on Eton, Burma and his first wife, Eileen O'Shaughnessy. It felt as if the narrative was moving forward rather than backwards from the publication of his final novel, *Nineteen Eighty-Four*, in an effort to explain how the great literary figure conjured Oceania, Newspeak, Big Brother etc. into existence. Of Orwell at Eton they say: 'However sardonic his tone ... however aloof in spirit ... he did not *not* enjoy himself' there (Stansky and Abrahams 1972: 119). Of his first wife, they comment perceptively: 'One cannot emphasise too strongly the importance of Eileen O'Shaughnessy in the life of Eric Blair' (1979: 110). The pages spent outlining O'Shaughnessy's life, before meeting Blair, is an indication of the significance of their relationship for the authors. As is their recognition of the importance of her brother, Laurence, in Eileen's life.

REFLECTIONS

Last year, feeling rather pleased with myself, I published some 'original research' about Orwell's Scottish ancestry. I posited that John Blair (1668-1728) was a survivor of the failed Darien Scheme (Dobson 2011) who washed ashore in Jamaica, subsequently becoming a slave-owner and the genesis of the family's wealth (Moore 2019b). While reviewing the biographies for information about Orwell's ancestors, I had neglected to consult *The Unknown Orwell* (1972). Stansky and Abrahams had hypothesised, nearly half-a-century ago, the Blairs '*might* also have been associated with the abortive Scottish Darien scheme in Panama of 1698' (ibid: 6). There were no supporting references or footnotes; the information appears to have been gleaned from interviews conducted by the authors with family, friends and acquaintances and could not be verified.

The contemporary ease of access to Orwell's total literary and journalistic output makes research a fundamentally different proposition for scholars today compared with what confronted Stansky and Abrahams half-a-century ago. Reflecting on the nature of the written versus spoken word, one can see that Stansky and Abrahams's experience of interviewing Orwell's friends, acquaintances, colleagues and family was crucial to the success of their biographies. Indeed, listening to twenty-six hours of the unedited, unpublished conversations recorded for a CBC Radio series (Wadhams 1983) provided for me a richer understanding than the published excerpts I had already read in print (Wadhams 1984). A greater sense of the person emerged as I was able to evaluate the impact of dialect, diction, tone and confidence with which individuals answered, or avoided, questions from the interviewer. Some were clearly more informed than others. Social class, so fundamental to understanding Orwell (and Britain), was much more easily detected when listening to the interviewees. As Americans, Stansky believes that their outsider status was useful in having their interviewees speak freely (Stansky 2019).

RE-EVALUATION

Despite the challenges faced in publishing these biographies, or perhaps due to them, Stansky and Abrahams produced pioneering work on George Orwell. Many of those I asked about their impressions of these first biographies came up with compliments such as 'well-written', 'intelligent', 'pioneering', 'concise' and 'illuminating'. Professor Richard Lance Keeble, editor of *George Orwell Studies*, feels 'Stansky and Abrahams's seminal texts, with their wealth of psychological insights and original research, remain crucial resources for all Orwellian researchers' while Dennis Glover, author of *The Last Man in Europe* (2018) notes 'a ring of freshness about them that comes from original research and making connections, rather than reassembling other peoples' findings, which can become a tedious exercise' (email correspondence 2019). Quite ironically, there was a general consensus that the challenging context in which the biographies were written has partly helped keep them relevant for scholars and the more general reader.

Stansky, a highly-credentialed and accomplished historian, certainly had the skills and aptitudes that helped make the two volumes of biography distinctive. *The New York Times*'s obituary (5 June 1998) for William 'Billy' Abrahams celebrated a poet, as well as a novelist, and credited the 'distinguished book editor … with almost single-handedly preserving the short story as a viable genre' and presiding over the annual O. Henry short story awards 'for more than three decades'. Stansky's expertise in British intellectual and political history, Abrahams's editorial skill crafting a narrative and perhaps, their outsiders' eyes, helped the Americans to portray George Orwell more successfully than many expected.

Orwell, in his essay, 'Why I Write', originally published in the short-lived journal *Gangrel* in 1946, says:

> I do not think one can assess a writer's motives without knowing something of his early development. His subject-matter will be determined by the age he lives in – at least this is true in tumultuous, revolutionary ages like our own – but before he ever begins to write he will have acquired an emotional attitude from which he will never completely escape (Orwell 1998 [1946]: 318).

Indeed, Stansky and Abrahams's pioneering biographies emphasise the seminal importance of Orwell's early life to understanding his literary development.

REFERENCES

Alldritt, Keith (1969) *The Making of George Orwell: An Essay in Literary History*, New York: St. Martin's Press

Atkins, John (1971) *George Orwell: A Literary Study*, London: Calder & Boyers

Beadle, Gordon B. (1973) Book review: *The Unknown Orwell*, *The Journal of Modern History*, Vol. 45, No. 4, December pp 701-703

Bowker, Gordon (2003) *Inside George Orwell*, New York: Palgrave Macmillan

Brander, Laurence (1954) *George Orwell*, London: Longmans, Green & Co

Buddicom, Jacintha (2006 [1974]) *Eric and Us*, Finlay Publishers, postscript edition

Colls, Robert (2013) *George Orwell: English Rebel*, Oxford: Oxford University Press

Connolly, Cyril (1972) Such were the joys, *New York Times*. Available online at https://www.nytimes.com/1972/11/12/archives/such-were-the-joys-such-were-the-joys.html, accessed on 8 July 2019

Connolly, Cyril (2008 [1938]) *Enemies of Promise*, Chicago: University of Chicago Press

Crick, Bernard (1992 [1980]) *George Orwell: A Life*, Harmondsworth, Middlesex: Penguin, second edition

Crick, Bernard (1989) *Essays on Politics and Literature*, Edinburgh: Edinburgh University Press

Cushman, Thomas and Rodden, John (eds) (2004) *George Orwell: Into the Twenty-First Century*, Boulder: Paradigm

Dobson, David (2011) *Scots in Jamaica, 1655-1855*, Baltimore: Clearfield

Fyvel, T. R. (1959) George Orwell and Eric Blair: Glimpses of a dual life, *Encounter*, Vol. 13, No. 1, July

Heppenstall, Rayner (1960) *Four Absentees*, London: Barrie & Rockliff

Heppenstall, Rayner (1981) A blurred portrait – Crick's Orwell, *Encounter*, February pp 77-79. Available online at https://www.unz.com/print/Encounter-1981feb-00077, accessed on 11 July 2019

Hollis, Christopher (1956) *A Study of George Orwell: The Man and His Works*, Michigan: Hollis and Carter

Hopkinson, Tom (1953) *George Orwell*, London: Longmans Green

Hynes, Samuel (1980) The unhappy vicar, *London Review of Books*, Vol. 2, No. 1, 24 January pp 26-28. Available online at https://www.lrb.co.uk/v02/n01/samuel-hynes/the-unhappy-vicar, accessed on 5 July 2019

Lewis, Jeremy (2012) *Cyril Connolly: A Life*, London: Pimlico

Jellinek, R. (1972) How Eric Blair became George Orwell, *New York Times*. Available online at https://www.nytimes.com/1972/11/12/archives/the-unknown-orwell-by-peter-stansky-and-william-abrahams.html, accessed on 5 July 2019

Koestler, Arthur (1980) A blurred portrait, *Observer*, 23 January

Meyers, Jeffrey (2000) *Orwell: Wintry Conscience of a Generation*. New York: W. W. Norton & Co.

Meyers, Jeffrey (2010) *Orwell: Life and Art*, Illinois: University of Illinois Press

Milton, Edith (1980) A mass of contradictions, *Christian Science Monitor*, 9 June. Available online at https://www.csmonitor.com/1980/0609/060955.html, accessed on 5 July 2019

Moore, Darcy (2018) Orwell and the appeal of opium, *George Orwell Studies*, Vol. 3, No.1 pp 83-102

Moore, Darcy (2019a) Orwell in Paris, *George Orwell Studies*, Vol. 3, No. 2 pp 55-69

Moore, Darcy (2019b) Orwell's Scottish ancestry & slavery', *Darcy Moore's Blog*. Available online at http://www.darcymoore.net/2019/06/23/orwells-scottish-ancestry-slavery/, accessed on 5 July 2019

Orwell, George (1968) *The Collected Essays, Journalism and Letters of George Orwell, Vols I - 4*, Orwell, Sonia and Angus, Ian (eds.) London: Secker & Warburg

Orwell, George (1998 [1943-1944]) *I Have Tried to Tell the Truth: 1943-1944, The Complete Works of George Orwell, Vol. 16*, Davison, Peter (ed.) London: Secker & Warburg

Orwell, George (1998 [1945]) *I Belong to the Left: 1945, The Complete Works of George Orwell, Vol. 17*, Davison, Peter (ed.) London: Secker & Warburg

Orwell, George (1998 [1946]) *Smothered in Journalism: 1946, The Complete Works of George Orwell, Vol. 18*, Davison, Peter (ed.) London: Secker & Warburg

Orwell, George (1998 [1949-1950]) *Our Job is to Make Life Worth Living: 1949-1950, The Complete Works of George Orwell, Vol. 20*, Davison, Peter (ed.) London: Secker & Warburg

Potts, Paul (1960) *Dante Called You Beatrice*, London: Eyre & Spottiswoode

Rees, Richard (1961) *Fugitive from the Camp of Victory*, London: Secker & Warburg

Rodden, John (2009) *George Orwell: The Politics of Literary Reputation*, London: Routledge

Sedgwick, Peter (1972) The unknown Orwell, *Socialist Worker*, 11 November. Available online at https://www.marxists.org/archive/sedgwick/1972/11/orwell.htm, accessed on 5 July 2019

Shelden, Michael (1991) *Orwell: The Authorised Biography*, London: Heinemann

Spender, Stephen (1972) The truth about Orwell, *New York Review of Books*. Available online at https://www.nybooks.com/articles/1972/11/16/the-truth-about-orwell/, accessed on 5 July 2019

Stansky, Peter (2003) Warts and all, *Literary Review*. June. Available online at https://literaryreview.co.uk/warts-and-all, accessed on 5 July 2019

Stansky, Peter (2019) Interview (via Skype), 13 July

Stansky, Peter and Abrahams, William (1966) *Journey to the Frontier: Two Roads to the Spanish Civil War*, Boston: Atlantic-Little, Brown

Stansky, Peter and Abrahams, William (1972) *The Unknown Orwell*, New York: Alfred A. Knopf

Stansky, Peter and Abrahams, William (1979) *Orwell: The Transformation*, New York: Alfred A. Knopf

Stansky, Peter and Abrahams, William (2019) *The Unknown Orwell and Orwell: The Transformation*, Audible: Peter Stansky

Taylor, D. J. (2004) *Orwell: The Life*, London: Vintage

Wadhams, Stephen (1983) *Unpublished Recordings from CBC Radio* (courtesy of the Orwell Society)

Wadhams, Stephen (1984) *Remembering Orwell*, Harmondsworth, Middlesex: Penguin

Williams, Raymond (1971) *Orwell*, London: Fontana

Winegarten, Renée (1980) Orwell: The transformation, October. Available online at https://www.commentarymagazine.com/articles/orwell-the-transformation-by-peter-stansky-and-william-abrahams, accessed on 5 July 2019

Woodcock, George (1967) *The Crystal Spirit: A Study of George Orwell*, London: Jonathan Cape

NOTE ON THE CONTRIBUTOR

Darcy Moore is a deputy principal at a secondary school in New South Wales. He teaches English and History and has worked as an academic in post-graduate teacher education at the University of Wollongong. His interest in Orwell began at school, thirty-seven years ago, when he was enthralled by *Animal Farm* and *Nineteen Eighty-Four*. He is currently working on a book, *Orwell in Paris*. He blogs at darcymoore.net and his Twitter handle is @Darcy1968. His Orwell collection can be accessed at darcymoore.net/orwell-collection/.

LETTER

Masha Karp Answers Her Critic

Dear Editor,

I think I should respond to Alexis Pogorelskin's review of my Russian biography of Orwell (*George Orwell Studies*, Vol. 4, No. 1, 2019) because it inadvertently misleads Western readers about the state of Orwell Studies in Russia. She reproaches my book for the absence of 'Russian scholarship on Orwell', which she finds 'missing, yet exceedingly desirable' and deplores the fact that the biography lacks 'a listing of major Russian books on Orwell'. I am sorry to disappoint Alexis Pogorelskin: when I was writing my book, there was hardly any 'Russian scholarship on Orwell' to speak of — and there is not much of it today.

This is not really surprising if one remembers that Orwell's own books, *Animal Farm* and *Nineteen Eighty-Four*, were first officially published in the Soviet Union only in 1988 and were greeted as welcome signs of Gorbachev's *perestroika*. Translations of other works of Orwell started appearing in the 1990s and 2000s, but not everything has been translated even now — *The Road to Wigan Pier*, for example, has not yet been published in Russian.

As far as Russian books on Orwell's prose and journalism are concerned, the scholarship, as other biographers put it, 'is in an embryonic state'.[1] As to biographies, my book published in 2017 was followed in 2019 by two more studies of Orwell's life,[2] and yet even today 'a listing of major Russian books on Orwell', no matter how desirable, is a bit of wishful thinking.

If we talk about articles rather than books, then apart from a couple of serious pieces I mention in the preface to my biography,[3] we are left with either vicious attacks on Orwell written by Soviet critics or post-*perestroika* forewords and afterwords accompanying the publications, which heroically attempt to bridge a 40-70-years gap between the writer's time and ours. These articles, often riddled with factual mistakes, try to adapt Orwell to the post-Soviet reality and mostly reflect their authors' views on the Soviet past. Given the difficulty Russia is experiencing with its assessment of its recent history, the analysis of these approaches might be an interesting subject in itself, but the primary aim of my biography was to give Russian readers at least some understanding of the famous author, whom they had not known much about.

Pogorelskin, therefore, is right that I believe Russian material is 'of less interest to [my] Russian readership than the Western sources' — mostly unavailable in Russian, but I was rather surprised to discover that she thinks that the book's content boils down just to the sources used. There are plenty of books in English that use familiar sources but offer a new approach to well-known facts.

And a minor point that seems to have been missed. Alexis Pogorelskin is very unhappy with me using 'Starshiy Brat' as a translation for 'Big Brother'. She obviously has not noticed that *Nineteen Eighty-Four* is the only work of Orwell's where the quotes are not translated by me, but taken from the published translation, done by Victor Golyshev (it says so on p. 12), one of the finest translators from English into Russian living today. And although the other version, 'Bolshoy Brat', which is favoured by the reviewer, has also been used by some Russian translators, I definitely prefer Golyshev's. Why? Simply because its meaning 'older/elder brother' is the exact rendering of the English phrase 'big brother'. Take any dictionary – English or American, on-line or printed — they all say that and, in fact, one quite often hears people causally saying: 'my big brother', 'my little brother'. Obviously, Orwell's 'Big Brother' stands for much more, but when giving a name to his character Orwell, no doubt, had in mind this everyday meaning of the familiar phrase and his English readers did get it. Why should his Russian readers get something else?

NOTES

[1] Felshtinsky, Yu. and Chernyavsky, G. *Orwell*, Moscow: Molodaya Gvardia, 2019: 10. These authors mention just two books: one fully devoted to literary analysis of Orwell's works (Mosina, V., *Three Main Books of George Orwell*. Moscow: MPU, 1999); the other that combines literary and sociological analysis (Alexeev. A. N., *Orwell's Year*, St Petersburg: Stupeni, 2001)

[2] Nedoshivin, V., Moscow: AST, 2019 and Felshtinsky, Yu. and Chernyavsky, G., Moscow: Molodaya Gvardia, 2019

[3] See Masha Karp, Orwell and Russia, translated into English by Sara Jolly (with John Crowfoot), The Orwell Society *Journal*, No. 13, autumn 2018 pp 14-17

Masha Karp,
West Hampstead,
London

REVIEWS

A History of 1930s British Literature
Benjamin Kohlmann and Matthew Taunton (eds)
Cambridge University Press, Cambridge, 2019 pp 474
ISBN: 978 1 1084 7453 5

'The 1930s are again en vogue.' So begins *A History of 1930s British Literature*, a magnificent volume edited by Benjamin Kohlmann and Matthew Taunton. The editors point to a surge in recent journalistic writing drawing comparisons between our current age and that previous epoch. 'Turning back to the 1930s seems to exert the same morbid fascination as watching a car crash unfold in slow motion, a catastrophe that seems tragically inevitable but that could have been avoided by the historical actors involved' (p. 1). In their introductory chapter, 'The Long 1930s', the editors conceptualise the decade not simply as the end point of modernism or the beginning of mid-century, but rather as a period of 'profound and continuous transition' (p. 3). Indeed, the twenty-six contributions to the volume succinctly and successfully 'dislodge the perception of the 1930s as a short-lived and quickly regretted aberration', which also 'demonstrates the centrality and continuing vitality of 1930s literary culture well beyond the political instrumentalisations and presentist reductions that have so often hampered a fuller understanding of the decade' (p. 12). The volume achieves a delicate balance of depth and breadth, covering a seemingly expansive number of topics and themes that will engage both expert and general readers.

The volume is divided into four thematic sections. Part I, 'Mapping a New Decade: Geographies and Identities', 'explores the geographical contours of writing in the long 1930s – new views of the city and the countryside as well as of the constituent parts of the United Kingdom – before turning to the decade's radical investment in neglected and non-normative ... identities' (p. 8). A chapter by Kristin Bluemel highlights the importance of the regional and the rural, and destabilises a singular Englishness in the construction of national identity, while Emma Zimmerman focuses on metropolitan life to reveal the anxieties present in the urban uncanny. Contributions by Nick Hubble, Kristin Ewins and Glyn Salton-Cox explore class, gender and queerness in their respective chapters.

Part II, 'Media Histories and the Institutions of Literature', 'seeks to reassess literature's place within an evolving media ecology, where (since the nineteenth century) the cultural centrality of the printed word is challenged by film recorded sound, radio and telephony' (p. 9). The category of 'institutions' in this chapter is particularly broad and includes libraries, bookshops, educational institutions, radio and film. Chapters on paperback books and pamphlets by Vike Martina Plock and Peter Marks are particularly engaging. Rachel Potter's chapter on 'International PEN: Writers, Free Expression, Organisations', which describes the relationship between literature and politics in the 1930s, may be of interest to readers of this journal.

Part III, 'Commitment and Autonomy', moves beyond the pursuit of 'binaristic dichotomies between politics and art, or between left and right, this third part explores a diverse range of commitments – religious as well as political – and their interlocking rather than oppositional relation to forms of artistic experimentation' (p. 10). This section is perhaps the least thematically cohesive, but only because of its attempt to cover a multitude of topics and certainly not to the detriment of the volume as a whole. Leo Mellor's chapter on 'The Documentary Impulse' and its consideration of *The Road to Wigan Pier* categorises the 'travelogue as a catalogue of deprivation, and thus a call for political action...' (p. 262), a theme prevalent in Orwell's work as a whole. Perhaps one of the finest discussions of the intersection of politics and literature in the volume comes from Tyrus Miller's 'Representing Fascism in 1930s Literature', which brings together Wyndham Lewis, Nancy Mitford, W. H. Auden, Christopher Isherwood and Cecil Day-Lewis, among others.

Part IV, 'The Global 1930s: Conflict and Change', 'explores the shifting position of British literature in relation to the turbulent geopolitical events of the decade. A series of connected phenomena made writers viscerally aware of the international context in which they worked' (p. 11). Here, chapters on empire and its decline by Greg Barnhisel, Peter Kalliney and Laura Winkiel can be found alongside John Connor's contribution on Anglo-Soviet literary relations, and additional chapters dealing with past and future wars. Readers looking for George Orwell in this magisterial volume will not be disappointed, particularly in this final section. A chapter on 'Late Modernism and the Spanish Civil War' by Patricia Rae is perhaps of most interest to readers of this journal, but Orwell appears not infrequently throughout the whole of the text. Focusing on *Homage to Catalonia*, Rae highlights several hallmarks of late modernism in Orwell's work – the turn inward, evasion and substitution. Her approach to the work 'endorses the goal of the present volume: that we must "lengthen" our perspective on the 1930s to make sense of its literature. In particular, it presumes that writings about war, violence and sacrifice in the decade were not cut from whole cloth but from "refunctioned" discourses inherited from the First World War', looking ahead to the impact of Cold War politics and the reception of the Spanish civil war (p. 356). So Rae encourages similar reconsiderations of the literature of the period, pointing to opportunities with Hemingway's *For Whom the Bell Tolls*, John Cornford's 'Full Moon at Tierz' and Auden's 'Spain'. A contribution by Marina MacKay on 'Total War' explores writings of the interwar period that are 'shaped by violence both recalled and anticipated' (p. 362), focusing in part on Orwell's *Keep the Aspidistra Flying*, *Coming Up for Air* and *Homage to Catalonia*.

This volume will be of interest both to readers looking specifically for George Orwell and also to readers with a general interest in British literature of the interwar period. Benjamin Kohlmann and Matthew Taunton have brought together contributions that cover such a wide range of themes that there is little doubt that there is something here for everyone. The 1930s, as the editors point out, represent a complicated period of literary history: 'Indeed, George Orwell's judgement regarding the Spanish Civil War – that its "true history" cannot be written because any account of it will inevitably be a "partisan history" – could just as easily be applied to the literary period of the 1930s as a whole' (p. 2). Nevertheless, this volume both complicates and clarifies narratives of this conceptually tricky period to wonderful ends.

Thomas J. Sojka,
Boston University

If George Orwell Were Alive Today: On *Nineteen Eighty-Four* and the Thrust of Orwellian Satire

John Dale

Australian Scholarly Publishers, Victoria, 2019 pp 44

ISBN 978 1 9258 0187 3 (pbk)

'I think Dad would've been amused by Donald Trump in an ironic sort of way,' George Orwell's son, Richard Blair commented in 2017, 'He may have thought: "There goes the sort of man I wrote about all those years ago"' (Blair quoted in Lynskey 2019). What would Orwell have made of our current times – with Trump, the climate crisis, the terror, and post-truth politics? As Blair notes, there is a lot that he would recognise.

Indeed, how would Orwell be voting if he had not passed away in 1950? This is a captivating question. Norman Podhoretz asked it in 1983 (concluding that Orwell would align himself with the neo-conservatives); in 2013, Stuart Jeffries posed the question in the *Guardian* (he wondered whether Orwell would be working in a call centre and writing in defence of the welfare state). And it is one of the two questions that John Dale asks in this new, short essay. The second, and 'far more interesting' question that Dale explores is: 'What would *Nineteen Eighty-Four* be like if it were written today?' (p. 7).

Dale reflects on these questions over the course of ten short chapters which make up the 43-page-long pamphlet. Orwell's writing endures 70 years after his death, with continued relevance. As many have pointed out, multiple Orwellisms have infiltrated everyday life and pop culture, such as the TV programmes *Big Brother* and *Room 101*, or the tendency to describe dystopian fiction as 'Orwellian'.

Orwell writes that every line 'of serious work that I have written since 1936 has been written, directly or indirectly *against* totalitarianism and *for* democratic Socialism, as I understand it' (p. 2). And Dale praises Orwell's commitment to truth and his ability to speak out against totalitarianism. It is this sense of truthfulness, free speech, liberty, freedom of thought and the exchange of ideas that makes Orwell such an important figure in today's climate of post-truth politics and fake news. Orwell wrote truthfully about what was occurring in the Soviet Union and the millions who were dying in the Gulag, 'unlike many of his fellow writers on the left – Auden, Spender, Day-Lewis' (p. 4). This is why Dale's second question about *Nineteen Eighty-Four* is such an interesting one: what would Orwell be speaking out against today that our current day writers may not be addressing? (p. 7)

In Chapter 3, 'A Changing Britain', Dale focuses on the cultural changes that the country has undergone since *Nineteen Eighty-Four*'s publication in 1949, highlighting the large-scale immigration that occurred from the early 1950s to the late 1970s. Dale notes the 'massive social and cultural change' is one of the major differences between post-war Britain and the present day, and how 'Orwell failed to foresee that religious belief would prove such a strong force in the future' (p. 13). Dale argues that 'if Orwell were writing *Nineteen Eighty-Four* today, seventy years later, and set in a London of the near future, it would be the threat of religious fundamentalism that he would warn against' (p. 19). Dale then argues that 'Islamist theology as practised in countries such as Saudi Arabia, Sudan, Yemen and Iran is by very definition a totalitarian construct: a politico-religious system of absolute power where the state has no limit to its authority and regulates every aspect of public and private life' (p. 19). Dale sees Islamist theology as 'not simply a religion, but a complete cultural and political system' that enacts violence and oppression on those who speak out against in blasphemy or apostasy, seeing 'the strongest taboos for any writer in the West' as concerning the 'cultural and social pressures caused by large-scale immigration and, in particular, the spread of radical Islam' and 'criticism of Islamist extremism and beliefs' (pp 20, 30-31).

Dale uses the example of the violent reaction to the publication of Salman Rushdie's *The Satanic Verses* in 1989, which was seen by Iran's Supreme Leader Grand Ayatollah Khomeini as an insult to 'Islamic sanctity', calling for all 'zealous Muslims' to execute the British author. The fatwa actually resulted in the assassination of the Japanese translator, the stabbing of its Italian translator, the shooting of its Norwegian publisher and the burning to death of 35 guests at a Turkish hotel hosting its Turkish publisher (p. 22). This example is used to demonstrate the tabooed nature of critique of radical Islamic belief. And this, Dale argues, is the kind of prevailing orthodoxy that Orwell would have spoken out against if *Nineteen Eighty-Four* were written today, to 'warn that the dangers to democracy now come from a new direction and the writers of our time must do what Orwell did: face up to the truth and write fearlessly' (p. 40).

REVIEW

The length of this short essay naturally gives rise to a focused route of inquiry and so Dale does not engage with many other social and cultural changes that have shaped Britain since 1950. For example, the multinational technology companies Facebook and Google are only mentioned once, even though they have changed the ways in which individuals communicate and the ways in which political doctrine impacts on the personal and the private. Dale quotes Orwell: 'The totalitarian state tries to control the thoughts and emotions of its subjects at least as completely as it controls their actions' (p. 5). As Carole Cadwalladr, the *Guardian* journalist who in 2018 exposed the Facebook-Cambridge Analytica data scandal, details in her presentation at a *TED* Conference in April 2019, 'Facebook's role in Brexit – and the threat to democracy': 'Hate and fear are being sown online all across the world ... we know that there is this dark undertow that is connecting us all globally. And it is flowing via the technology platforms ... Our democracy is broken.' Cadwalladr calls Facebook 'the handmaidens to authoritarianism, that is on the rise all over the world' in their manipulation of advertising, data and their work with Cambridge Analytica (Cadwalladr 2019). Perhaps a lengthier study with more space to engage with the many changes that have shaped our contemporary society would have benefited the argument; for example, would Orwell have voted Leave or Remain in the UK referendum?

Furthermore, to claim that the critique of radical Islam is the 'strongest taboo' in the West neglects the extent of the

Islamophobia and scapegoating that is present within mainstream media and tabloid coverage, and the dangers to democracy that this rhetoric imposes. Michael Welsh's foreword to *Global Islamophobia: Muslims and Moral Panic in the West* (2016) outlines that across Western societies, 'Islamophobia manifests in various forms, most notably as resistance to immigration and asylum seeking', using the Australian government's removal of the word 'multiculturalism' from the title of its immigration service as an example, renaming the Department of Immigration, Multilateralism and Indigenous Affairs (DIMIA) the Department of Immigration and Citizenship (DIAC) (Welsh 2012: x). In 2018, the Home Affairs Select Committee of the House of Commons launched an inquiry into hate crime, looking at anti-Muslim sentiments in print media, with more than 40 stories on issues related to Islam and Muslims having been corrected in mainstream national newspapers in an 18-month period by Miqdaad Versi, the assistant secretary general of the Muslim Council of Britain (Versi 2018).

Sara Ahmed believes that multiculturalism 'has itself been sentenced to death: as if the act of welcoming diverse others has endangered the security and well-being of the nation'. Ahmed writes:

> … the language of fascism is written in the language of love. Love is made into the primary quality of attachment, what motivates individuals into fascism: 'We hate foreigners *because* we love our country.' … Love has an enormous political utility: transforming fascist subjects not only into heroic subjects, but also into potential or actual victims of crime as well as those who 'alone' are willing to fight crime. … If love is what binds, then it also involves what I have called an 'affective economy'. An affective subject of love is created, as various figures circulate, from bogus asylum seekers, to 'Islamic terrorists', as objects of hate, accumulating negative value (Ahmed 2013).

Indeed, for Winston Smith in *Nineteen Eighty-Four* it is in the Ministry of Love along with this feeling that equates to utter sublimation and political orthodoxy: 'He loved Big Brother' (Orwell 311). As well as being concerned about the danger to democracy that a theocratic regime imposes, I would like to believe that Orwell would also be wary of the ways in which politicians and the media harness language that engages in the 'affective economy' of othering, division and polarisation. Would Orwell have watched Trump's rallies and heard the cries and chants of 'Lock her up' and 'Send her back', and been struck by the similarity to *Nineteen Eighty-Four*'s Two Minute Hate sessions (Sorkin 2018)? I wonder whether, as well as being concerned over individual's rights in theocratic societies, Orwell would have also been wary of the 'language of love' as described by Ahmed that is often harnessed against religious or racial minorities.

Dale has asked two very interesting questions that have great critical weight for our current day politics and culture, presenting thought-provoking insights into Orwell's commitment to truth and political views. But they warrant a lengthier study into the manifold directions from which 'dangers to democracy now come', and also the ways in which these dangers clash, coalesce and operate in an affective economy of emotion (p. 4).

REFERENCES

Ahmed, Sara (2013) The bond of belief, *feministkilljoys*, August. Available online at https://feministkilljoys.com/2013/08/28/the-bond-of-belief/, accessed on 29 November 2019

Cadwalladr, Carole (2019) Facebook's role in Brexit – and the threat to democracy, *TED,* April. Available online at https://www.ted.com/talks/carole_cadwalladr_facebook_s_role_in_brexit_and_the_threat_to_democracy?language=en, accessed on 22 November 2019

Davidson Sorkin, Amy (2018) From 'Lock her up' to 'Send her back': Trump in North Carolina, *The New Yorker*, July. Available online at https://www.newyorker.com/news/daily-comment/from-lock-her-up-to-send-her-back-trump-in-north-carolina, accessed on 1 December 2019

Lynskey, Dorian (2019) Nothing but the truth: The legacy of George Orwell's *Nineteen Eighty-Four*, *Guardian*, 19 May. Available online at https://www.theguardian.com/books/2019/may/19/legacy-george-orwell-nineteen-eighty-four, accessed on 25 September 2019

Jefferies, Stuart (2013), What would George Orwell made of the world in 2013?, *Guardian*, 24 January 2013. Available online at https://www.theguardian.com/books/2013/jan/24/george-orwell-britain-in-2013, accessed on 24 September 2019

Orwell, George (1992 [1949]) *Nineteen Eight-Four*, New York: Random House

Podhoretz, Norman (2018) If Orwell were alive today, *Quadrant*, 27. October pp 48-53

Versi, Miqdaad (2018) Islamophobia not an issue in the British press? You've got to be kidding, *Guardian,* 27 April. Available online at https://www.theguardian.com/commentisfree/2018/apr/27/islamophobia-not-british-press-issue-got-to-be-kidding, accessed on 1 December 2019

Welsh, Michael (2012), Foreword, Morgan, George (ed.) *Global Islamophobia: Muslims and Moral Panic in the West,* New York: Routledge pp ix-xiv

REVIEW

Polly Hember,
Royal Holloway, University of London

Red Britain: The Russian Revolution in Mid-Century Culture
Matthew Taunton
Oxford University Press, Oxford, 2019 pp 320
ISBN: 978 0 19881 7710

For better or worse the Russian Revolution of 1917 still stands as one of, perhaps the most, famous case of radical social change. The revolutionary movement of the Bolsheviks represents a rupture in the fabric of capitalist historical continuance that reverberated and echoed throughout the twentieth century and which, with the collapse of the USSR, still impacts on contemporary politics today. For many it is a beacon of inspiration – the world was changed once and so it may be again, and there could be a future that is not simply more of the same grim capitalist present. On the other hand, for many others the 1917 revolution leads only to the horrors of the gulags, the show trials and the despotism of Stalinism.

All too easily, this debate about what the revolution may mean and does mean can collapse into binaries of condemnation or celebration but such reductive and ahistorical argument does little to advance understanding of the strengths and weaknesses of the Russian revolutionary movement. On top of this, in an epoch where to think of the future – of any kind of radical social and political change – is next to impossible, it becomes ever more vital to turn to the revolutionary moments of the past and draw from them resources for political struggle in the present.

Matthew Taunton's book serves an invaluable function, moving discussions about the Soviet revolution beyond a stale and moralistic binary whilst simultaneously providing rich insight into the ways in which the revolution was contested and responded to in a wide variety of cultural spheres by writers, journalists, legal theorists and cultural figures ranging from sympathetic communists to ardent defenders of the capitalist West. As Taunton writes in the 'Introduction', the revolution 'never secured the monopoly on the future' but at the same time 'its potential futurity can never be entirely extinguished' (p. 10). What is present, then, are the variety of questions that the seismic impact of the Russian revolution forced British culture to confront. The book's chapters work through a selection of these questions – from the issue of the future with which the book opens, to discussions of mathematics and law before finishing with a discussion about literacy.

The first chapter, 'The Radiant Future', opens with an anecdote regarding the trip to the Soviet Union taken by (among others) Kingsley Martin, editor of the *New Statesman and Nation*, and political cartoonist David Low. Strolling in the Park of Culture and Rest in Leningrad, in 1932, Low remarks that it 'might be the opening scene in one of Wells's Utopias!' British culture then, had to respond to the fact that the future not only could be transformed, but *had* been by the success of the Russian Revolution (p. 12). The opening sections of the chapter draw out the ways in which this tension played out through British culture, which often turned to the popular scientific fiction of H. G. Wells to describe what had happened. The social democrat turned ardent anti-communist, Arthur Koestler, compared Soviet workers to those who had journeyed on Wells's time machine, jumping from the seventeenth century all the way to the twentieth in the space of a decade or so. Wells himself is drawn into a futurological debate with G. K. Chesterton about 'socialist Russia in the present' (p. 20).

The value of this history is to place it within the larger context of Marxist, socialist and communist writing about the future. Taunton is right to point out that the English left generally avoided Utopian speculation even as *fin-de-siècle* and early twentieth century culture was full of Utopian speculation and possible futures. As the century advanced Wells found it harder to imagine a future distinct from Russia – before it may have been only a hypothetical but, with the emergence of the Soviet states, 'Wells's eye for the future had been blinded by a red light emanating from the East' (p. 22).

The struggle to imagine a future that was not in some way a response to the Soviet's found itself playing out throughout the first half of the century. Isaac Asimov saw Orwell's *Nineteen Eighty-Four* as sacrificing a plausible future world for a feud with Stalinism, while Huxley's *Brave New World* seemed to see the nightmare future in both hedonistic capitalism and Stalinist communism. The chapter explores this impact that the Soviet Union had on the idea of the future, but also offers some hugely insightful arguments into the ways in which, internal to the Soviet Union, there were also complex debates about the temporality of communism. The idea of the shining future, where present suffering would be offset by the emergence and construction of a socialist society, exerted a powerful influence. Taunton lists many writers who bought into this (even if they would later become less sympathetic or even antagonistic to Soviet communism) such as Bertrand Russell, George Bernard Shaw and Emma Goldman.

The section on the 'younger, subtler minds' who professed their belief in this notion of the future reward is particularly worth considering as Taunton shows the ways in which anti-capitalist thought could easily excuse the horrors of Stalinism in pursuit of the larger goal (p. 39). W. H. Auden's poem 'Spain', with its portentous lines of 'Tomorrow, perhaps the future' and 'the conscious acceptance of guilt in the necessary murder', is an excellent example of this mood finding cultural expression. 'Looking to the future the darkness of the present can be made meaningful and even morally necessary' (p. 41). It was that willingness to excuse violence and murder as morally necessary that led Orwell to his 'dismal view of the Auden circle' and his own repudiation of the radiant future ideal that Auden and many others were willing to uphold, even if only for a time (p. 45).

From the discussions about the future the next chapter turns to numbers, as the politics of a planned economy and calculative rationality became a 'key trope that mid-century writers – the mathematically knowledgeable as well as the ignorant – deployed as they reflected on the Russian Revolution' (p. 61). Statistics were everywhere in discussions of Soviet systems used by both those sympathetic and supportive and those opposed to centralised planning. (Parenthetically, it seems worth pointing out the ways in which statistics are still used today in discussions of actually existing socialism, especially by the political right). The seeming quantitative omniscience (to use Taunton's useful phrase) was, for many on the anti-communist right, something 'deeply off-putting' (p. 65). Malcolm Muggeridge and other romantic anti-communists recoiled from the 'supposed simple certainties of mathematics' (p. 65).

D. H. Lawrence is read as having a somewhat more sophisticated critique, objecting to a society that was *too* committed to equality, *too* invested in a quantitative assessment of human capability that dangerously elided the qualitative differences between individuals. For Lawrence, the Soviets had elevated the average man at the cost of 'complex artistic individuality' (p. 75). Nabakov is another writer who saw in the politics of maths a 'deadening Leninist egalitarianism' that needed to be countered with the upholding of aesthetic freedom and play (p. 80). Nabokov, drawing from the Russian literature of the nineteenth century, particularly in his early work, sought to counter a perceived revolutionary nihilism of quantification. Of course, to talk about the politics of numbers in this context necessitates a discussion of Orwell's famous dictum that 2+2=5.

Orwell was hugely influenced by Yevgeny Zamyatin's 1923 novel *We*, taking from the novel the notion that mathematical perfection is not the same thing as rationality. Zamyatin's character D-503 is haunted by the square root of minus one, the imaginary number with no real solution. Here, then, as Russian mathematicians were independently beginning to verify, was the possibility of a break with the 'rigid determinism of continuous functions' and because of this break the space emerges for 'free will' (p. 87). Thus, even in the society, which many saw as being mathematically ordered, there remains the possibility of difference and change.

The section of the chapter on *Nineteen Eighty-Four* is also fascinating. The much-quoted equation mentioned above forms a basis for a great deal of the political responses to the novel. For Marxists like Isaac Deutscher, Orwell clung to the rationality of

2+2=4 but in the wake of Stalinism and its purges could not think dialectically or grasp the totality of the historical moment because of his commitment to the stolid rationality of 2+2. Thus, the problem with Orwell is not a lack of Marxism, but an inability to be Marxist enough. The final sections of the chapter offer an overview of the Marxist approach to mathematics, from Engels's *Dialectic of Nature* and Anti-Duhrin to Alain Badiou's interest in reviving the higher mathematics. This section includes a fascinating introduction to the world of Soviet mathematicians and figures such as David Haden Guest, the British mathematician and communist who called for a Mathematical Philosophy that would be rigorously Marxist but who died in the Spanish civil war before any such lofty goal could be realised.

From there the book moves on to a discussion of the law, followed by a chapter on the changes in agriculture. These chapters, like the previous two, capture all the strengths of the book, with a huge range of material marshalled to put forward a compelling and richly layered exploration of the issue. The final chapter, with the provocative title 'The Compensations of Illiteracy', explores the relationship between writing and orality, particularly in a cultural context that was commonly illiterate. In the reports of many visitors to Russia it seems that 'in spite of Marxism-Leninism's profession of a dogmatic atheism, the Soviet state had shaped itself to imitate the Church' through its use of the written word (p. 219).

Stephen Graham, who visited Russia in the early 1900s, saw it as a culture of sound, not writing, exemplified by the chanting in Orthodox cathedrals and churches. In contrast, England with its Protestant individualism had developed a literary individualism that reflected this religious move and so in the sociability of Russian culture Graham sees 'a rosy picture of medieval Britain' (p. 222). This High-Church oral tradition could easily be seen as being threatened by the literate urbanism of the Bolshevik movement – a point made by John Maynard Keynes who saw the communist revolutionaries as an 'ascetic Protestant sect' (p. 227). In a far-too-short aside, Taunton connects this to the writing of Hewlett Johnson, the 'red Dean of Canterbury' who argued that Bolshevism was explicitly justifiable in Christian terms.

Given the links the book seeks to make between writing and political theology, it is a small oversight that no mention is made of the work of Marxists such as Roland Boer who have shown how Marxist thought, even within the Soviet Union, had a complex and ambiguous relationship to the theological. However, the point is well made that only by extending 'our analysis beyond the binary opposition between secular and religious' can we begin to account more accurately for the role and function of political religion (p. 231).

In a British context, the orality of communism heralded an opportunity for reviving an 'oral-aural sociality that had been swept aside by the Allied forces of capitalism' (p. 232). The Popular Front poets such as Jack Lindsay are seen as embodying and promulgating a 'phonocentric communism' that would see a communist recovery of a lost English way of life (p. 234). This folk-communism would later become of great importance to the New Left as it sought to outline a compelling socialist vision that could move beyond or against the horror of Stalinism. The orality of the communist culture was also noted by anti-communists. Writers such as Arthur Koestler saw the sloganeering and propagandising, as well the need to avoid political misspeaking, as a 'degeneration into primitive orality' which inescapably leads to an impoverishment of thought (p. 239).

This also intersects with emergent technology, as Taunton points out the ways that Stalin in particular masterfully utilised the telegram and telephone to spread his voice across the entire nation. In the post-war period the (im)possibility of dialogue became a pressing concern, highlighted by Taunton through an excellent section on Doris Lessing's *The Golden Notebook* (1962). Lessing is read as working through a more open formal dialogic structure, echoing a need to 'create space for forms of socialist commitment outside' the Communist Party (p. 255).

At the book's conclusion, Taunton differentiates his own position *vis-à-vis* the development of social being and the interaction of culture and politics. Differing with Raymond Williams that 'consciousness is fully capable of determining social being', the book sees culture and politics as 'dynamically and dialogically interrelated' (p. 265). Or to put it another way, they are dialectically linked (which allows for a refusal of a binary between social being determining consciousness and *vice versa*). In the overlapping spheres of economics, law, literature and futurology Taunton puts forward a rich and compelling narrative that shows just how radically challenging the Russian Revolution was and still should be. This invaluable piece of scholarship wears its learning lightly, using a dizzying array of sources and literary references to provide a compelling and essential read for all who are interested in the radical rupture of capitalist hegemony that the Russian Revolution represented.

Jonathan Greenaway,
Manchester Metropolitan University

On *Nineteen Eighty-Four*: A Biography
D. J. Taylor
Abrams Press, New York, 2019 pp 208
ISBN: 978 1 4197 3800 5

George Orwell's *Nineteen Eighty-Four* was first published in June of 1949. The immediate sensation that followed can hardly be overstated. Within a month, further printings were necessary in the US as the novel was selected for the Book of the Month Club. Within three months, by the end of August, the first of many adaptations was produced. The swiftness involved in this transition is unthinkable in today's terms, particularly given the respected and venerable name of its star: David Niven graced the airwaves as Winston Smith. Such a move is indicative not only of the novel's obvious success, but of its capacity for growth and change: for life. In a matter of weeks, *Nineteen Eighty-Four* was brimming with sufficient *élan vital* to strain at the bounds of Orwell's authorial jurisdiction. It is not unreasonable, in light of the sense of immortality that Orwell's most famous work evokes, to feel – when confronted with a conventional biography of Orwell – that an ending precipitated by the author's death is insufficient. In many respects, the story had just begun.

It is upon this sense that D.J. Taylor capitalises throughout *On Nineteen Eighty-Four: A Biography*. Refusing to limit himself to the life of Orwell, Taylor instead charts the life – or the 'meteoric flight' – of his most enduring work. Dividing the book into three sections (succinctly titled 'Before', 'During', and 'After'), Taylor briskly addresses key historical, literary and biographical influences upon Orwell's novel; the long process of composition; and an examination of its afterlife from the Cold War to the present day (p. 114).

Inevitably, the first and second sections – dealing primarily with Orwell's life in a manner not dissimilar to a conventional biography – will feel familiar to the Orwell aficionado. Taylor is aware that many readers will come to this book with foreknowledge, replete with such mental images as 'a tall, spindly man in wretched health, smouldering cigarette in one hand, hunched over a typewriter in a stuffy, badly heated bedroom while outside the North Atlantic wind lashes against the windows' (p. 168). As a result, there is an unavoidable sense that the ground on which Taylor walks is sometimes a little well-worn. Prior biographers (among whom Taylor himself stands as a respected member) have covered details including, for example, *Nineteen Eighty-Four*'s remarkable sales figures, which Taylor recapitulates at length (p. 110). On the other hand, of course, it has been around sixteen years since the last biography of Orwell was published (with the obvious exception of Dorian Lynskey's recent *The Ministry of Truth*, against which Taylor's volume will inevitably be compared). As a consequence, it is entirely appropriate to readdress key moments in the genesis and composition of *Nineteen Eighty-Four*.

This is not to say that Taylor doesn't bring anything new to the table in these early sections of the book. He provides a characteristically readable and accessible account of some of the novel's key influences, reminding us, for example, of the wide range of dystopian literature which influenced Orwell, including *The Iron Heel* (1908), *When the Sleeper Wakes* (1907), *Brave New World* (1932) and *The Secret of the League* (1907) (p. 42). Where the opening section really shines, however, is in Taylor's analysis of Orwell's earlier novels. Though he is not the first to suggest that there is a relationship to be found between *Nineteen Eighty-Four* and the quartet of novels written by Orwell in the 1930s, Taylor offers up some interesting evidence for cohesion and foreshadowing in his handling of the latter. He suggests, for example, that even the name of *Keep the Aspidistra Flying*'s (1936) protagonist, Gordon Comstock, 'turns out to prefigure one of the truncations of Newspeak ("Comstock" = "Common Stock")' (p. 21). In so doing, Taylor performs the important work of using the prestige of *Nineteen Eighty-Four* to buoy up – rather than eclipse – the early novels which have seen far less popular and critical attention, potentially introducing them to a new audience and challenging Orwell's own belief that these works were simply failures.

It is the third part of this book, however, that proves the most valuable contribution to commentary on Orwell's dystopia. Transcending the constraint of Orwell's death, Taylor is able to meditate on the book's continuing legacy, from the immediate backlash as various political camps attempted to claim the work for themselves, to the recent spike in sales and usage of the term 'Orwellian' in connection with the advent of Brexit and the election of Donald Trump (p. 163). Not only does this section provide nuanced and reflective considerations of those present-day circumstances in which it is and is not appropriate to evoke Orwell's doom-laden date, but an emphasis on the afterlife of the novel opens the door to under-considered subject matter. Taylor is able, for example, to turn his attention to the many film, television, radio and stage adaptations of *Nineteen Eighty-Four*, in addition to its place in popular music (p. 154). With the notable exception of 2018's *George Orwell on Screen*, to which Taylor acknowledges having early access, there has been no significant or sustained analysis of the important place these adaptations hold in the history of the novel. It is in these details that the real value of constructing a biography of the novel as opposed to the author becomes apparent: Taylor is able to extend his reach beyond Orwell, just as *Nineteen Eighty-Four* has done itself.

Christopher Hitchens has warned that, in any discussion of *Nineteen Eighty-Four*, omitting the context in which Orwell wrote robs us of what he calls an 'extra dimension'. Taylor's book retains this dimension while adding another, charting the course of the novel's long and flourishing life and facilitating fresh interpretive pathways, while checking the ever-present evocation of Orwell's novel in the face of a huge variety of recent political events. Bernard Crick argues that *Nineteen Eighty-Four* is 'misread if not read in the context of its time'. Taylor's *On Nineteen Eighty-Four: A Biography* wisely reminds us that its time is not yet up.

Daniel Buckingham,
University of Birmingham

George Orwell Studies

Subscription information
Each volume contains two issues, published half-yearly.

Annual Subscription (including postage)

Personal Subscription

UK	£30
Europe	£33
RoW	£35

Institutional Subscription

UK	£100
Europe	£115
RoW	£120

Single Issue copies (subject to availability)

UK	£15
Europe	£17
RoW	£20

Enquiries regarding subscriptions and orders should be sent to:

> Journals Fulfilment Department
> Abramis Academic
> ASK House
> Northgate Avenue
> Bury St Edmunds
> Suffolk, IP32 6BB
> UK

Tel: +44(0)1284 700321
Email: info@abramis.co.uk

www.ingramcontent.com/pod-product-compliance
Lightning Source LLC
Chambersburg PA
CBHW080404170426
43193CB00016B/2807